ᐃᓂᓂᐧᐊᐠ ᐁᐧᐸ ᐃᓂᓂᐧᐊᐠ, ᐃᐅᑐᖏᑯᕉᐧᐃᐁᐧ ᐁᐧᐸ ᐃᐅᑐᖏᑯᕉᐧᐃᐁᐧ

PEOPLE TO PEOPLE, NATION TO NATION

À L'AUBE D'UN RAPPROCHEMENT

ᕆᐸᑦᑖᓂᕊᑐᐃᔭᖏ ᕆᐸᑦᑖᖮᑐᐃᔭᖏ, ᐃᔪᕀᕆᓂᐟ ᐃᔪᕀᕆᖮᐟ

HIGHLIGHTS FROM THE
REPORT OF THE ROYAL COMMISSION ON ABORIGINAL PEOPLES

Canadian Cataloguing in Publication Data

Canada. Royal Commission on Aboriginal Peoples.
People to people, nation to nation:
Highlights from the report of the Royal Commission on Aboriginal Peoples.

Issued also in French under the title:
À l'aube d'un rapprochement.
Issued also in Cree and Inuktitut.

ISBN 0-662-25044-3
Cat. no. Z1-1991/1-6E

1. Native peoples – Canada.
2. Native peoples – Canada – Social conditions.
3. Native peoples – Canada – Economic conditions.
4. Native peoples – Canada – Politics and government.
I. Title.
II. Title: Highlights from the Report of the
    Royal Commission on Aboriginal Peoples

E78.C2R46 1996   971'.00497   C96-980366-4

CONTENTS

NOTE TO READERS

This book introduces you to some of the main themes and conclusions in the final report of the Royal Commission on Aboriginal Peoples. That report is a complete statement of the Commission's opinions on, and proposed solutions to, the many complex issues raised by the 16-point mandate set out by the government of Canada in August 1991.

It was not possible to include in this book the great wealth of information, analysis, proposals for action and recommendations that appear in the report. Each of its five volumes presents the Commission's thoughts and recommendations on a range of interconnected issues. Chapters are devoted to major topics such as treaties, economic development, health, housing, Métis perspec-

tives, and the North. Volume 5 draws all the recommendations together in an integrated agenda for change. The five volumes are entitled

1. Looking Forward, Looking Back
2. Restructuring the Relationship
3. Gathering Strength
4. Perspectives and Realities
5. Renewal: A Twenty-Year Commitment

The five chapters in this book correspond to the five volumes of the report.

THE ROYAL COMMISSION
ON ABORIGINAL PEOPLES

CO-CHAIRS

René Dussault, j.c.a.

Georges Erasmus

COMMISSIONERS

Paul L.A.H. Chartrand

J. Peter Meekison

Viola Robinson

Mary Sillett

Bertha Wilson

A Word from Commissioners

Canada is a test case for a grand notion – the notion that dissimilar peoples can share lands, resources, power and dreams while respecting and sustaining their differences. The story of Canada is the story of many such peoples, trying and failing and trying again, to live together in peace and harmony.

But there cannot be peace or harmony unless there is justice. It was to help restore justice to the relationship between Aboriginal and non-Aboriginal people in Canada, and to propose practical solutions to stubborn problems, that the Royal Commission on Aboriginal Peoples was established. In 1991, four Aboriginal and three non-Aboriginal commissioners were appointed to investigate the issues and advise the government on their findings.

We began our work at a difficult time.

■ It was a time of anger and upheaval. The country's leaders were arguing about the place of Aboriginal people in the constitution. First Nations were blockading roads and rail lines in Ontario and British Columbia. Innu families were encamped in protest of military installations in Labrador. A year earlier, armed conflict between Aboriginal and non-Aboriginal forces at Kanesatake (Oka) had tarnished Canada's reputation abroad – and in the minds of many citizens.

■ It was a time of concern and distress. Media reports had given Canadians new reasons to be disturbed about the facts of life in many Aboriginal communities: high rates of poverty, ill health, family break-down and suicide. Children and youth were most at risk.

■ It was also a time of hope. Aboriginal people were rebuilding their ancient ties to one

> There can be no peace
> or harmony
> unless there is justice.

another and searching their cultural heritage for the roots of their identity and the inspiration to solve community problems.

We directed our consultations to one overriding question: *What are the foundations of a fair and honourable relationship between the Aboriginal and non-Aboriginal people of Canada?*

We held 178 days of public hearings, visited 96 communities, consulted dozens of experts, commissioned scores of research studies, reviewed numerous past inquiries and reports. Our central conclusion can be summarized simply: *The main policy direction, pursued for more than 150 years, first by colonial then by Canadian governments, has been wrong.*

Successive governments have tried – sometimes intentionally, sometimes in ignorance – to absorb Aboriginal people into Canadian society, thus eliminating them as distinct peoples. Policies pursued over the decades have undermined – and almost erased – Aboriginal cultures and identities.

This is assimilation. It is a denial of the principles of peace, harmony and justice for which this country stands – and it has failed. Aboriginal peoples remain proudly different.

Assimilation policies failed because Aboriginal people have the secret of cultural survival. They have an enduring sense of themselves as peoples with a unique heritage and the right to cultural continuity.

This is what drives them when they blockade roads, protest at military bases and occupy sacred grounds. This is why they resist pressure to merge into Euro-Canadian society – a form of cultural suicide urged upon them in the name of 'equality' and 'modernization'.

Assimilation policies have done great damage, leaving a legacy of brokenness affecting Aboriginal individuals, families and communities. The damage has been equally serious to the spirit of Canada – the spirit of generosity and mutual accommodation in which Canadians take pride.

Yet the damage is not beyond repair. The key is to reverse the assumptions of assimilation that still shape and constrain Aboriginal life chances – despite some worthy reforms in the administration of Aboriginal affairs.

To bring about this fundamental change, Canadians need to understand that *Aboriginal peoples are nations.* That is, they are political and cultural groups with values and lifeways distinct from those of other Canadians. They lived as nations – highly centralized, loosely federated, or small and clan-based – for thousands of years before the arrival of Europeans. As nations, they forged trade and military alliances among themselves and with the new arrivals. To this day, Aboriginal people's sense of confidence and well-being as individuals remains tied to the strength of their nations. Only as members of restored nations can they reach their potential in the twenty-first century.

Let us be clear, however. To say that Aboriginal peoples are nations is not to say that they are nation-states seeking independence from Canada. They are collectivities with a long shared history, a right to govern themselves and, in general, a strong desire to do so in partnership with Canada.

The Commission's report is an account...

...of the relationship between Aboriginal and non-Aboriginal people that is a central facet of Canada's heritage.

...of the distortion of that relationship over time.

...of the terrible consequences of distortion for Aboriginal people – loss of lands, power and self-respect.

We hope that our report will also be a guide

to the many ways Aboriginal and non-Aboriginal people can begin – right now – to repair the damage to the relationship and enter the next millennium on a new footing of mutual recognition and respect, sharing and responsibility.

LOOKING FORWARD, LOOKING BACK

1

After some 500 years of a relationship that has swung from partnership to domination, from mutual respect and co-operation to paternalism and attempted assimilation, Canada must now work out fair and lasting terms of coexistence with Aboriginal people.

THE STARTING POINT

The Commission has identified four compelling reasons to do so:

- Canada's claim to be a fair and enlightened society depends on it.
- The life chances of Aboriginal people, which are still shamefully low, must be improved.
- Negotiation, as conducted under the current rules, has proved unequal to the task of settling grievances.
- Continued failure may well lead to violence.

Canada as a Fair and Enlightened Society

Canada enjoys a reputation as a special place – a place where human rights and dignity are guaranteed, where the rules of liberal democracy are respected, where diversity among peoples is celebrated. But this reputation represents, at best, a half-truth.

A careful reading of history shows that Canada was founded on a series of bargains with Aboriginal peoples – bargains this country has never fully honoured. Treaties between Aboriginal and non-Aboriginal governments were agreements to share the land. They were replaced by policies intended to

...remove Aboriginal people from their homelands.

The foundations
of a fair and
equitable relationship
were laid in our
early interaction.

...suppress Aboriginal nations and their governments.

...undermine Aboriginal cultures.

...stifle Aboriginal identity.

It is now time to acknowledge the truth and begin to rebuild the relationship among peoples on the basis of honesty, mutual respect and fair sharing. The image of Canada in the world and at home demands no less.

The Life Chances of Aboriginal People

The third volume of our report, *Gathering Strength*, probes social conditions among Aboriginal people. The picture it presents is unacceptable in a country that the United Nations rates as the best place in the world to live.

Aboriginal people's living standards have improved in the past 50 years – but they do not come close to those of non-Aboriginal people:

■ Life expectancy is lower.

■ Illness is more common.

■ Human problems, from family violence to alcohol abuse, are more common too.

■ Fewer children graduate from high school.

■ Far fewer go on to colleges and universities.

■ The homes of Aboriginal people are more often flimsy, leaky and overcrowded.

■ Water and sanitation systems in Aboriginal communities are more often inadequate.

■ Fewer Aboriginal people have jobs.

■ More spend time in jails and prisons.

Aboriginal people do not want pity or hand-outs. They want recognition that these problems are largely the result of loss of their lands and resources, destruction of their economies and social institutions, and denial of their nationhood.

They seek a range of remedies for these injustices, but most of all, they seek control of their lives.

Failed Negotiations

A relationship as complex as the one between Aboriginal and non-Aboriginal people is necessarily a matter of negotiation. But the current climate of negotiation is too often rife with conflict and confrontation, accusation and anger.

Negotiators start from opposing premises. Aboriginal negotiators fight for authority and resources sufficient to rebuild their societies and exercise self-government – as a matter of right, not privilege. Non-Aboriginal negotiators strive to protect the authority and resources of Canadian governments and look on transfers to Aboriginal communities as privileges they have bestowed.

Frequent failure to come to a meeting of minds has led to bitterness and mistrust among Aboriginal people, resentment and apathy among non-Aboriginal people.

In our report, we recommend four principles for a renewed relationship – to restore a positive climate at the negotiating table – and a new political framework for negotiations. We discuss the principles at the end of this chapter and the new framework in Chapter 2.

Risk of Violence

Aboriginal people have made it clear, in words and deeds, that they will no longer sit quietly by, waiting for their grievances to be heard and their rights restored. Despite their long history of peacefulness, some leaders fear that violence is in the wind.

What Aboriginal people need is straightforward, if not simple:

- control over their lives in place of the well-meaning but ruinous paternalism of past Canadian governments
- lands, resources and self-chosen governments with which to reconstruct social, economic and political order
- time, space and respect from Canada to heal their spirits and revitalize their cultures

Canada can be a diverse, exciting, productive, caring country...a country where every child has an equal opportunity to grow up full of hope and enthusiasm for the future.
> Martha Flaherty
> President, Pauktuutit Inuit Women's Organization

We are getting sick and tired of the promises of the federal government. We are getting sick and tired of Commissions. We are getting sick and tired of being analyzed... We want to see action.
> Norman Evans
> Pacific Metis Federation

The Ghosts of History

Every Canadian will gain if we escape the impasse that breeds confrontation between Aboriginal and non-Aboriginal people across barricades, real or symbolic. But the barricades will not fall until we understand how they were built.

Studying the past tells us who we are and where we came from. It often reveals a cache of secrets that some people are striving to keep hidden and others are striving to tell. In this case, it helps explain how the tensions between Aboriginal and non-Aboriginal people came to be, and why they are so hard to resolve.

Canadians know little about the peaceful and co-operative relationship that grew up between First Peoples and the first European visitors in the early years of contact. They know even less about how it changed, over the centuries, into something less honourable. In our report, we examine that history in some detail, for its ghosts haunt us still.

The ghosts take the form of dishonoured treaties, theft of Aboriginal lands, suppression of Aboriginal cultures, abduction of Aboriginal children, impoverishment and disempowerment of Aboriginal peoples. Yet at the beginning, no one could have predicted these results, for the theme of early relations was, for the most part, co-operation.

The relationship between Aboriginal and non-Aboriginal people evolved through four stages:

- There was a time when Aboriginal and non-Aboriginal people lived on separate continents and knew nothing of one another.
- Following the years of first contact, fragile relations of peace, friendship and rough equality were given the force of law in treaties.
- Then power tilted toward non-Aboriginal people and governments. They moved Aboriginal people off much of their land and took steps to 'civilize' and teach them European ways.
- Finally, we reached the present stage – a time of recovery for Aboriginal people and cultures, a time for critical review of our relationship, and a time for its renegotiation and renewal.

Many of today's malfunctioning laws and institutions – the *Indian Act* and the break-up of nations into bands, to name just two – are remnants of the third stage of our history. But there was honour in history, too; indeed, the foundations of a fair and equitable relationship were laid in our early interaction.

STAGE 1:
SEPARATE WORLDS

Before 1500, Aboriginal societies in the Americas and non-Aboriginal societies in Europe developed along separate paths, in ignorance of one another. The variety in their languages, cultures and social traditions was enormous. Yet on both sides of the Atlantic, independent peoples with evolving systems of government – though smaller and simpler than the nations and governments we know today – flourished and grew.

In the southeastern region of North America, the Cherokee were organized into a confederacy of some 30 cities – the greatest of which was nearly as large as imperial London when English explorers first set eyes on it. Further south, in

America, separated from Europe by a wide ocean, was inhabited by a distinct people, divided into separate nations, independent of each other and the rest of the world, having institutions of their own, and governing themselves by their own laws. It is difficult to comprehend... that the discovery of either by the other should give the discoverer rights in the country discovered which annulled the previous rights of its ancient possessors.

Chief Justice
John Marshall
United States
Supreme Court
Worcester v. *Georgia* (1832)

Central and South America, Indigenous peoples
had carved grand empires out of the mountains
and jungles long before Cortez arrived.

In northern North America, Aboriginal cultures were shaped by environment and the evolu-
tion of technology:

- The plentiful resources of sea and forest
  enabled west coast peoples to build societies
  of wealth and sophistication.
- On the prairies and northern tundra,
  Aboriginal peoples lived in close harmony
  with vast, migrating herds of buffalo and
  caribou.
- In the forests of central Canada,
  Aboriginal peoples harvested wild rice
  from the marshes and grew corn, squash
  and beans beside the river banks, supple-
  menting their crops by fishing, hunting
  and gathering.
- On the east coast and in the far north, the
  bounty of the sea and land – and their own
  ingenuity – enabled Aboriginal peoples to
  survive in harsh conditions.

The Americas were not, as the Europeans told
themselves when they arrived, *terra nullius* –
empty land.

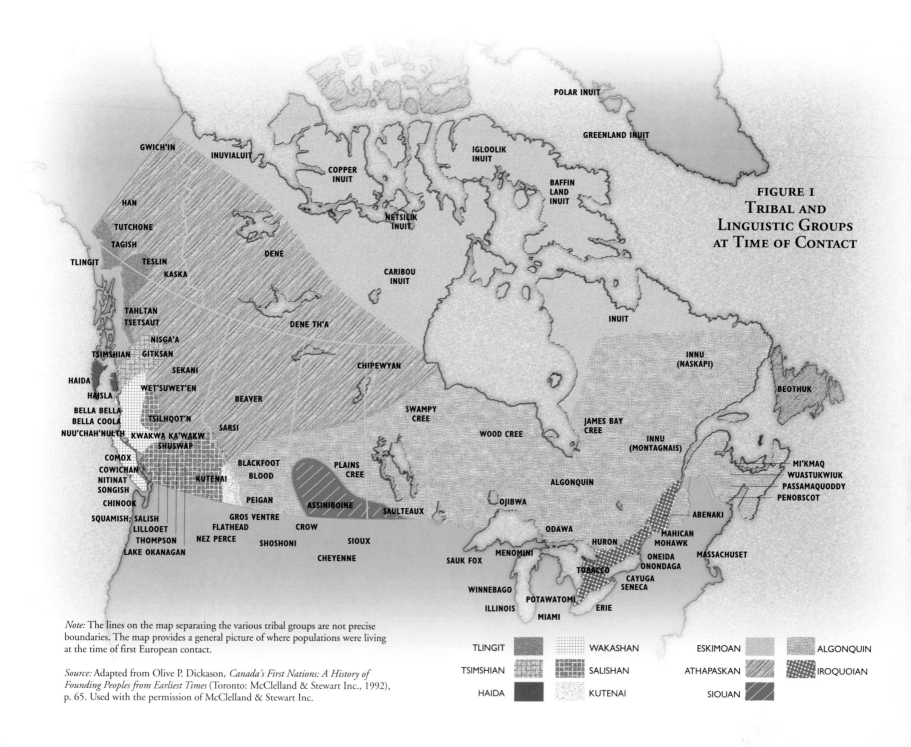

FIGURE I
TRIBAL AND
LINGUISTIC GROUPS
AT TIME OF CONTACT

POLAR INUIT

GREENLAND INUIT

GWICH'IN
INUVIALUIT
COPPER INUIT
IGLOOLIK INUIT
BAFFIN LAND INUIT
HAN
TUTCHONE
TAGISH
DENE
NETSILIK INUIT
TLINGIT
TESLIN
KASKA
CARIBOU INUIT
INUIT
INNU (NASKAPI)
TAHLTAN
TSETSAUT
DENE TH'A
NISGA'A
TSIMSHIAN
GITKSAN
SEKANI
CHIPEWYAN
BEOTHUK
HAIDA
WET'SUWET'EN
HAISLA
BEAVER
BELLA BELLA
BELLA COOLA
TSILHQOT'N
SWAMPY CREE
NUU'CHAH'NULTH
SARSI
JAMES BAY CREE
INNU (MONTAGNAIS)
KWAKWA KA'WAKW
SHUSWAP
WOOD CREE
COMOX
MI'KMAQ
COWICHAN
KUTENAI
BLACKFOOT
BLOOD
PLAINS CREE
WUASTUKWIUK
NITINAT
PASSAMAQUODDY
SONGISH
ALGONQUIN
PENOBSCOT
PEIGAN
CHINOOK
ASSINIBOINE
SAULTEAUX
OJIBWA
ABENAKI
SQUAMISH; SALISH
GROS VENTRE
LILLOOET
FLATHEAD
CROW
ODAWA
MAHICAN
THOMPSON
NEZ PERCE
HURON
MOHAWK
LAKE OKANAGAN
SHOSHONI
SIOUX
MASSACHUSET
MENOMINI
ONEIDA
ONONDAGA
CHEYENNE
TOBACCO
CAYUGA
SAUK FOX
SENECA
WINNEBAGO
POTAWATOMI
ERIE
ILLINOIS
MIAMI

Note: The lines on the map separating the various tribal groups are not precise boundaries. The map provides a general picture of where populations were living at the time of first European contact.

Source: Adapted from Olive P. Dickason, *Canada's First Nations: A History of Founding Peoples from Earliest Times* (Toronto: McClelland & Stewart Inc., 1992), p. 65. Used with the permission of McClelland & Stewart Inc.

TLINGIT	WAKASHAN	ESKIMOAN	ALGONQUIN
TSIMSHIAN	SALISHAN	ATHAPASKAN	IROQUOIAN
HAIDA	KUTENAI	SIOUAN	

Stage 2:
Nation-to-Nation Relations

Encounters between Aboriginal and non-Aboriginal people began to increase in number and complexity in the 1500s. Early contact unfolded roughly as follows:

- Mutual curiosity and apprehension.
- An exchange of goods, tentative at first, then expanding steadily.
- Barter and trade deals, friendships and inter-marriage, creating bonds between individuals and families.
- Military and trade alliances, creating bonds between and among nations.

Non-Aboriginal accounts of early contact tend to emphasize the 'discovery' and 'development' of North America by explorers from Europe. But this is a one-sided view. For at least 200 years, the newcomers would not have been able to survive the rigours of the climate, succeed in their businesses (fishing, whaling, fur trading), or dodge each other's bullets without Aboriginal help.

Cautious co-operation, not conflict, was the theme of this period, which lasted into the eighteenth or nineteenth century, depending on the region. For the most part, Aboriginal and non-Aboriginal people saw each other as separate, distinct and independent. Each was in charge of its own affairs. Each could negotiate its own military alliances, its own trade agreements, its own best deals with the others.

Co-operation was formalized in two important ways:

- In treaties, which were set down in writing by British, French and other European negotiators and solemnized by Aboriginal nations in oral and visual records, including wampum belts.
- In the extraordinary document known as the *Royal Proclamation of 1763*.

Treaty Making

Treaty making among Aboriginal peoples dates back to a time long before Europeans arrived. Aboriginal nations treated among themselves to establish peace, regulate trade, share use of lands and resources, and arrange mutual defence.

Whereas it is just and reasonable, and essential to Our Interests and the Security of Our Colonies, that the several Nations or Tribes of Indians, with whom we are connected and who live under Our Protection, should not be molested or disturbed in the Possession of such parts of Our Dominions and Territories as, not having been ceded to or purchased by Us, are reserved for them, or any of them, as their Hunting Grounds...
Royal Proclamation of 1763

Through pipe smoking and other ceremonies, they gave these agreements the stature of sacred oaths.

European traditions of treaty making date to Roman times, but in the seventeenth century, they took on new importance. They became the means for the newborn states of Europe to control their bickering and warfare – indeed, to end it for long periods. Treaties were a way of recognizing each other's independence and sovereignty and a mark of mutual respect.

In the colonies that became Canada, the need for treaties was soon apparent. The land was vast, and the colonists were few in number. They feared the might of the Aboriginal nations surrounding them. Colonial powers were fighting wars for trade and dominance all over the continent. They needed alliances with Indian nations.

The British colonial government's approach to the treaties was schizophrenic. By signing, British authorities appeared to recognize the nationhood of Aboriginal peoples and their equality as nations. But they also expected First Nations to acknowledge the authority of the monarch and, increasingly, to cede large tracts of land to British control – for settlement and to protect it from seizure by other European powers or by the United States.

The Aboriginal view of the treaties was very different. They believed what the king's men told them, that the marks scratched on parchment captured the essence of their talks. They were angered and dismayed to discover later that what had been pledged in words, leader to leader, was not recorded accurately. They accepted the monarch, but only as a kind of kin figure, a distant 'protector' who could be called on to safeguard their interests and enforce treaty agreements. They had no notion of giving up their land, a concept foreign to Aboriginal cultures.

The Two Row Wampum, a belt commemorating a 1613 treaty between the Mohawk and the Dutch, captures the understanding of Aboriginal peoples – treaties were statements of

Over several hundred years, treaty making has been used to keep the peace and share the wealth of Canada.

peace, friendship, sharing or alliance, not submission or surrender:

> A bed of white wampum symbolizes the purity of the agreement. There are two rows of purple, and those two rows represent the spirit of our ancestors. Three beads of wampum separating the two purple rows symbolize peace, friendship and respect. The two rows of purple are two vessels travelling down the same river together. One, a birch bark canoe, is for the Indian people, their laws, their customs and their ways. The other, a ship, is for the white people and their laws, their customs and their ways. We shall each travel the river together, side by side, but in our own boat. Neither of us will try to steer the other's vessel.

The Royal Proclamation

The *Royal Proclamation of 1763* was a defining document in the relationship between Aboriginal and non-Aboriginal people in North America. Issued in the name of the king, the proclamation summarized the rules that were to govern British dealings with Aboriginal people – especially in relation to the key question of land.

It is a complex legal document, but the central messages of the proclamation are clear in its preamble. Aboriginal people were not to be "molested or disturbed" on their lands.

Transactions involving Aboriginal land were to be negotiated properly between the Crown and "assemblies of Indians". Aboriginal lands were to be acquired only by fair dealing: treaty, or purchase by the Crown.

The proclamation portrays Indian nations as autonomous political entities, living under the protection of the Crown but retaining their own internal political authority. It walks a fine line between safeguarding the rights of Aboriginal peoples and establishing a process to permit British settlement. It finds a balance in an arrangement allowing Aboriginal and non-Aboriginal people to divide and share sovereign rights to the lands that are now Canada.

More than a hundred years later, in 1867, the arrangement we know as Confederation would also allow for power sharing among diverse peoples and governments. But the first confederal bargain was with First Peoples.

STAGE 3:
RESPECT GIVES WAY TO
DOMINATION

In the 1800s, the relationship between
Aboriginal and non-Aboriginal people began to
tilt on its foundation of rough equality. The
number of settlers was swelling, and so was their
power. As they dominated the land, so they came
to dominate its original inhabitants. They gained
power as a result of four changes that were transforming the country:

1. The population mix was shifting to favour
   the settlers. Immigration continued to add
   to their numbers, while disease and poverty
   continued to diminish Aboriginal nations.
   By 1812, immigrants outnumbered
   Indigenous people in Upper Canada by a
   factor of ten to one.

2. The fur trade was dying, and with it the old
   economic partnership between traders and
   trappers. The new economy was based on
   timber, minerals, agriculture. It needed land
   – not labour – from Aboriginal people, who
   began to be seen as 'impediments to
   progress' instead of valued partners.

3. Colonial governments in Upper and Lower

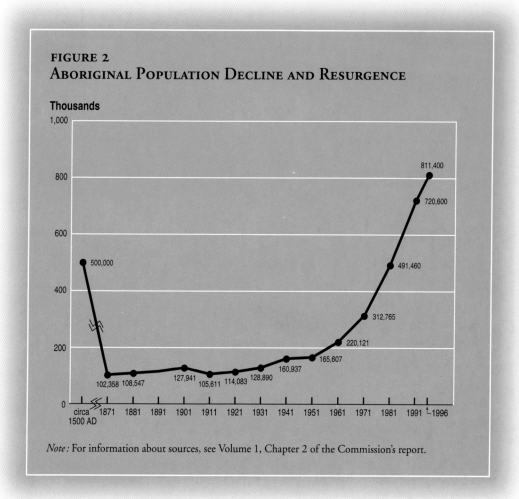

FIGURE 2
ABORIGINAL POPULATION DECLINE AND RESURGENCE

Note: For information about sources, see Volume 1, Chapter 2 of the Commission's report.

History has not been written yet from the Indian point of view.
Violet Soosay
Montana First Nation community
Hobbema, Alberta

[The *Indian Act*] has...deprived us of our independence, our dignity, our self-respect and our responsibility.
Kaherine June Delisle
Kanien'kehaka First Nation
Kahnawake, Quebec

Canada no longer needed Aboriginal nations as military allies. The British had defeated all competitors north of the 49th parallel. South of it, the United States had fought for self-government and won. The continent was at peace.

4. An ideology proclaiming European superiority over all other peoples of the earth was taking hold. It provided a rationale for policies of domination and assimilation, which slowly replaced partnership in the North American colonies. These policies increased in number and bitter effect on Aboriginal people over many years and several generations.

Ironically, the transformation from respectful coexistence to domination by non-Aboriginal laws and institutions began with the main instruments of the partnership: the treaties and the *Royal Proclamation of 1763*. These documents offered Aboriginal people not only peace and friendship, respect and rough equality, but also 'protection'.

Protection was the leading edge of domination. At first, it meant preservation of Aboriginal lands and cultural integrity from encroachment by settlers. Later, it meant 'assistance', a code

word implying encouragement to stop being Aboriginal and merge into the settler society.

Protection took the form of compulsory education, economic adjustment programs, social and political control by federal agents, and much more. These policies, combined with missionary efforts to civilize and convert Indigenous people, tore wide holes in Aboriginal cultures, autonomy and feelings of self-worth.

Policies of Domination and Assimilation

No Canadian acquainted with the policies of domination and assimilation wonders why Aboriginal people distrust the good intentions of non-Aboriginal people and their governments today.

■ Colonial and Canadian governments established 'reserves' of land for Aboriginal people – usually of inadequate size and resources – with or without treaty agreements. The system began in 1637, with a Jesuit settlement at Sillery in New France. Reserves were designed to protect Aboriginal people and preserve their ways, but operated instead to isolate and impoverish them.

■ In 1857, the Province of Canada passed an act to "Encourage the Gradual Civilization of the

The Doctrine
of Assimilation

THE DOCTRINE OF ASSIMILATION was based
on four dehumanizing (and incorrect) ideas
about Aboriginal peoples and their cultures:

- that they were inferior peoples
- that they were unable to govern themselves and that colonial and Canadian
  authorities knew best how to protect their
  interests and well-being
- that the special relationship of respect and
  sharing enshrined in the treaties was an
  historical anomaly with no more force or
  meaning
- that European ideas about progress and
  development were self-evidently correct
  and could be imposed on Aboriginal people without reference to any other values
  and opinions – let alone rights – they
  might possess

Indian Tribes". It provided the means for Indians
"of good character" (as determined by a board of
non-Aboriginal examiners) to be declared, for all
practical purposes, non-Indian. As non-Indians,
they were invited to join Canadian society, bringing a portion of tribal land with them. Only one
man, Elias Hill, a Mohawk from the Six Nations,
is known to have accepted the invitation.

■ By the beginning of the nineteenth century, significant numbers of Métis people were
living in almost all parts of Canada. Their heritage of Aboriginal, French and British cultures,
combined with their experience as intermediaries
between the factions competing for trade and territory, resulted in their emergence as distinct peoples with their own culture, institutions and
lifeways.

But British and Canadian policy toward
Métis people was dismissive. They were not
'Indians', and they were not legitimate settlers.
The usual practice was to declare them 'squatters'
and edge them off the land they were farming
when preferred settlers moved in.

Under Louis Riel, the Métis of the Red River
Valley struggled for their own land and govern-

The promises we have to make to you
are not for today only, but for
tomorrow, and not only for you but
for your children born and unborn.
And the promises we make will be
carried out as long as the sun shines
above and the water flows in the
ocean.

Alexander Morris,
Lieutenant Governor of
Manitoba and the
North-West Territories
Address to the Cree and
Salteaux, Fort Qu'Appelle
(1874)

ment. They were promised both in the *Manitoba Act* of 1870, but those promises were later denied. Many moved further west and north, where they again fought for land and political recognition. In the spring of 1885 their forces were crushed at Batoche by a military expedition sent by Ottawa. The people were dispersed again, and to this day, their claims for a secure land base and their own forms of government have not been settled.

■ Confederation, declared in 1867, was a new partnership between English and French colonists to manage lands and resources north of the 49th parallel. It was negotiated without reference to Aboriginal nations, the first partners of both the French and the English. Indeed, newly elected Prime Minister John A. Macdonald announced that it would be his government's goal to "do away with the tribal system, and assimilate the Indian people in all respects with the inhabitants of the Dominion."

■ The *British North America Act*, young Canada's new constitution, made "Indians, and

Lands reserved for the Indians" a subject for government regulation, like mines or roads. Parliament took on the job with vigour – passing laws to replace traditional Aboriginal governments with band councils with insignificant powers, taking control of valuable resources located on reserves, taking charge of reserve finances, imposing an unfamiliar system of land tenure, and applying non-Aboriginal concepts of marriage and parenting.

These laws, and others, were codified in the Indian Acts of 1876, 1880, 1884 and later. The Department of the Interior (later, Indian Affairs) sent Indian agents to every region to see that the laws were obeyed.

■ In 1884, the potlatch ceremony, central to the cultures of west coast Aboriginal nations, was outlawed. In 1885, the sun dance, central to the cultures of prairie Aboriginal nations, was outlawed. Participation was a criminal offence.

■ In 1885, the Department of Indian Affairs instituted a pass system. No outsider could come onto a reserve to do business with an Aboriginal resident without permission from the Indian agent. In many places, the directives were interpreted to mean that no Aboriginal person could leave the reserve without permission from the Indian agent. Reserves were beginning to resemble prisons.

In 1849, the first of what would become a network of residential schools for Aboriginal children was opened in Alderville, Ontario. Church and government leaders had come to the conclusion that the problem (as they saw it) of Aboriginal independence and 'savagery' could be solved by taking children from their families at an early age and instilling the ways of the dominant society during eight or nine years of residential schooling far from home.

Attendance was compulsory. Aboriginal languages, customs and habits of mind were suppressed. The bonds between many hundreds of Aboriginal children and their families and nations were bent and broken, with disastrous results.

During this stage in the changing relationship, Canadian governments moved Aboriginal communities from one place to another at will. If Aboriginal people were thought to have too little food, they could be relocated where game was more plentiful or jobs might be found. If they

were suffering from illness, they could be relocated to new communities where health services, sanitary facilities and permanent housing might be provided. If they were in the way of expanding agricultural frontiers, or in possession of land needed for settlement, they could be relocated 'for their own protection'. If their lands contained minerals to be mined, forests to be cut, or rivers to be dammed, they could be relocated 'in the national interest'.

■ In each world war, more than 3,000 registered Indians and unrecorded numbers of Inuit, Métis and non-status Indian people volunteered for the Canadian Armed Forces. Their contributions of life, limb and money were appreciated at home, and most of the volunteers found acceptance on the battlefield. Hundreds lost their lives there or were wounded.

Those who survived asked for no special honours, but they expected to be treated as other war veterans were on their return to Canada. They were not. They were denied many of the benefits awarded to other vets. Land was taken from their reserves and used 'for military purposes' or awarded to non-Aboriginal veterans. Those left alive today are still seeking recognition for their part in the war effort and compensation for their later losses.

◼ Treaties were still the chosen means of managing the relationship. But the treaty process was increasingly strained by conflicting interpretations of their purpose.

The purpose of the treaties, in Aboriginal eyes, was to work out ways of sharing lands and resources with settlers, without any loss of their own independence. But the representatives of the Crown had come to see the treaties merely as a tool for clearing Aboriginal people off desirable land.

To induce First Nations to sign, colonial negotiators continued to assure them that treaty provisions were not simply agreed, but *guaranteed* to them – for as long as the sun shone and the rivers flowed.

STAGE 4:
RENEWAL AND RENEGOTIATION

Policies of domination and assimilation battered Aboriginal institutions, sometimes to the point of collapse. Poverty, ill health and social disorganiza-tion grew worse. Aboriginal people struggled for survival as individuals, their nationhood erased from the public mind and almost forgotten by themselves.

Resistance to assimilation grew weak, but it never died away. In the fourth stage of the relationship, it caught fire and began to grow into a political movement. One stimulus was the federal government's White Paper on Indian policy, issued in 1969.

The White Paper proposed to abolish the *Indian Act* and all that remained of the special relationship between Aboriginal people and Canada – offering instead what it termed *equality*. First Nations were nearly unanimous in their rejection. They saw this imposed form of 'equality' as a coffin for their collective identities – the end of their existence as distinct peoples. Together with with Inuit and Métis, they began realize the full significance of their survival in the face of sustained efforts to assimilate them. They began to see their struggle as part of a worldwide human rights movement of Indigenous peoples. They began to piece together the legal case for their continuity as peoples – nations within Canada – and to speak out about it.

They studied their history and found evidence confirming that they have rights arising

The fact is that when the settlers came, the Indians were there, organized in societies and occupying the land as their forefathers had done for centuries. This is what Indian title means...

Supreme Court of Canada
Calder v. *Attorney General of British Columbia* (1973)

from the spirit and intent of their treaties and the *Royal Proclamation of 1763*. They took heart from decisions of Canadian courts, most since 1971, affirming their special relationship with the Crown and their unique interest in their traditional lands. They set about beginning to rebuild their communities and their nations with new-found purpose.

The strong opposition of Aboriginal people to the White Paper's invitation to join mainstream society took non-Aboriginal people by surprise. The question of who Aboriginal people are and what their place is in Canada became central to national debate.

A dozen years of intense political struggle by Aboriginal people, including appeals to the Queen and the British Parliament, produced an historic breakthrough. "Existing Aboriginal and treaty rights" were recognized in the *Constitution Act, 1982*.

This set the stage for profound change in the relationship among the peoples of Canada, a change that most governments have nevertheless found difficult to embrace.

THE WAY FORWARD

The policies of the past have failed to bring peace and harmony to the relationship between Aboriginal peoples and other Canadians. Equally, they have failed to bring contentment or prosperity to Aboriginal people.

In poll after poll, Canadians have said that they want to see justice done for Aboriginal people, but they have not known how. In the following chapters, we outline a powerful set of interlinked ideas for moving forward.

In the years since the White Paper, Canadian governments have been prodded into giving Aboriginal communities more local control. They have included more Aboriginal people in decision making and handed over bits and pieces of the administrative apparatus that continues to shape Aboriginal lives.

But governments have so far refused to recognize the continuity of Aboriginal nations and the need to permit their decolonization at last. By their actions, if not their words, governments continue to block Aboriginal nations from assuming the broad powers of governance that would permit them to fashion their own institutions and work out their own solutions to social,

We propose four principles as the basis for a renewed relationship: recognition, respect, sharing and responsibility.

economic and political problems. It is this refusal that effectively blocks the way forward.

The new partnership we envision is much more than a political or institutional one. It must be a heartfelt commitment among peoples to live together in peace, harmony and mutual support.

For this kind of commitment to emerge from the current climate of tension and distrust, it must be founded in visionary principles. It must also have practical mechanisms to resolve accumulated disputes and regulate the daily workings of the relationship.

We propose four principles as the basis of a renewed relationship.

1 Recognition

The principle of mutual recognition calls on non-Aboriginal Canadians to recognize that Aboriginal people are the original inhabitants and caretakers of this land and have distinctive rights and responsibilities flowing from that status. It calls on Aboriginal people to accept that non-Aboriginal people are also of this land now, by birth and by adoption, with strong ties of love and loyalty. It requires both sides to acknowledge and relate to one another as partners, respecting each other's laws and institutions and co-operating for mutual benefit.

2 Respect

The principle of respect calls on all Canadians to create a climate of positive mutual regard between and among peoples. Respect provides a bulwark against attempts by one partner to dominate or rule over another. Respect for the unique rights and status of First Peoples, and for each Aboriginal person as an individual with a valuable culture and heritage, needs to become part of Canada's national character.

3 Sharing

The principle of sharing calls for the giving and receiving of benefits in fair measure. It is the basis on which Canada was founded, for if Aboriginal peoples had been unwilling to share what they had and what they knew about the land, many of the newcomers would not have lived to prosper. The principle of sharing is central to the treaties and central to the possibility of real equality among the peoples of Canada in the future.

4 Responsibility

Responsibility is the hallmark of a mature relationship. Partners in such a relationship must be accountable for the promises they have made, accountable for behaving honourably, and accountable for the impact of their actions on the well-being of the other. Because we do and always will share the land, the best interests of Aboriginal and non-Aboriginal people will be served if we act with the highest standards of responsibility, honesty and good faith toward one another.

We propose that treaties be the mechanism for turning principles into practice. Over several hundred years, treaty making has been used to keep the peace and share the wealth of Canada. Existing treaties between Aboriginal and non-Aboriginal people, however dusty from disuse, contain specific terms that even now help define the rights and responsibilities of the signatories toward one another.

We maintain that new and renewed treaties can be used to give substance to the four principles of a just relationship. How they can be used is explained in Chapter 2.

The Six Nations of the Iroquois Confederacy have described the spirit of the relationship as they see it in the image of a silver covenant chain. "Silver is sturdy and does not easily break," they say. "It does not rust and deteriorate with time. However, it does become tarnished. So when we come together, we must polish the chain, time and again, to restore our friendship to its original brightness."
Chief Jacob E. Thomas
Cayuga First Nation
Haudenosaunee (Iroquois)
Confederacy

Restructuring the Relationship

2

To restore the essence of the early relationship between Aboriginal and settler societies described in Chapter 1, the elements of partnership must be recreated in modern form. The starting point for this transformation is recognition of Aboriginal nationhood.

Aboriginal Peoples as Nations

The arguments for recognizing that Aboriginal peoples are nations spring from the past and the present. They were nations when they forged military and trade alliances with European nations. They were nations when they signed treaties to share their lands and resources. And they are nations today – in their coherence, their distinctiveness and their understanding of themselves.

Recognition of Aboriginal nationhood poses no threat to Canada or its political and territorial integrity. Aboriginal nations have generally sought coexistence, co-operation and harmony in their relations with other peoples. What they seek from Canada now is their rightful place as partners in the Canadian federation.

This chapter shows how the foundations of Aboriginal nationhood were undone and how they can be rebuilt.

The Case for Self-Government

Aboriginal people trace their existence and their systems of government back as far as memory and oral history extend. They say that the ulti-

Aboriginal Governments and the Canadian Charter of Rights and Freedoms

SOME PEOPLE HAVE EXPRESSED a fear that Aboriginal governments might be able to use their right of self-government to exempt themselves from the *Canadian Charter of Rights and Freedoms*. The Commission reviewed evidence on both sides of this question and concluded that the Charter does apply to Aboriginal governments.

However, the constitution allows federal and provincial governments to use a 'notwithstanding' clause to step outside the Charter in certain circumstances. Recognized Aboriginal governments should also be free to exercise this option.

Conflict could arise, for example, between Aboriginal and treaty rights on one hand and the Charter on the other. Section 25 of the *Constitution Act, 1982* allows for a flexible interpretation of the Charter that, in effect, gives primacy to Aboriginal and treaty rights. This means that Aboriginal governments should have considerable leeway in designing laws reflecting their cultures, traditions and values.

The constitution does not allow Aboriginal governments to deny the equality rights of women. Those rights are guaranteed to all women without exception.

mate source of their right to be self-governing is the Creator. The Creator placed each nation on its own land and gave the people the responsibility of caring for the land – and one another – until the end of time.

Three other sources of the right of self-government apply to Aboriginal peoples:

- In international law, which Canada respects, all peoples have a right of self-determination. Self-determination includes governance, so Indigenous peoples are entitled to choose their own forms of government, within existing states.
- In Canadian history, the colonial powers won no 'rights of conquest', for there was no conquest. Nor was North America *terra nullius,* free for the taking, as was claimed later. In most of their early dealings with Indigenous peoples in what is now Canada, the colonial powers recognized them as self-governing nations – codifying their recognition in treaties and in the *Royal Proclamation of 1763*.

■ Aboriginal peoples' right of self-government within Canada is acknowledged and protected by the constitution. It recognizes that Aboriginal rights are older than Canada itself and that their continuity was part of the bargain between Aboriginal and non-Aboriginal people that made Canada possible.

Aboriginal nations have accepted the need for power sharing with Canada. In return, they ask Canadians to accept that Aboriginal self-government is not, and can never be, a 'gift' from an 'enlightened' Canada. The right is *inherent* in Aboriginal people and their nationhood and was exercised for centuries before the arrival of European explorers and settlers. It is a right they never surrendered and now want to exercise once more.

We believe Aboriginal people must be recognized as partners in the complex arrangements that make up Canada. Indeed, we hold that Aboriginal governments are *one of three orders of government in Canada* – federal, provincial/territorial, and Aboriginal. The three orders are autonomous within their own spheres of jurisdiction, thus sharing the sovereignty of Canada as a whole. Aboriginal governments are not like municipal governments, which exercise powers delegated from provincial and territorial governments.

Shared sovereignty is an important feature of Canadian federalism. It permitted the early partnership between Aboriginal and non-Aboriginal people, and later it permitted the union of provinces that became Canada.

Canadian governments are coming gradually to accept the idea of shared sovereignty and Aboriginal self-government. But they have been loath to hand over the full range of powers needed by genuinely self-governing nations or the resources needed to make self-government a success.

REBUILDING ABORIGINAL NATIONS

We have concluded that the right of self-government cannot reasonably be exercised by small, separate communities, whether First Nations, Inuit or Métis. It should be exercised by groups

AN ABORIGINAL NATION should be defined as a sizeable body of Aboriginal people that possesses a shared sense of national identity and constitutes the predominant population in a certain territory or collection of territories.

Thus, the Mi'kmaq, the Innu, the Anishnabe, the Blood, the Haida, the Inuvialuit, the western Métis Nation and other peoples whose bonds have stayed at least partly intact, despite government interference, are nations. There are about 1,000 reserve and settlement communities in Canada, but there are 60 to 80 Aboriginal nations.

Self-government is a right they never surrendered and that they want to exercise once more.

of a certain size – groups with a claim to the term 'nation'.

The problem is that the historical Aboriginal nations were undermined by disease, relocations and the full array of assimilationist government policies. They were fragmented into bands, reserves and small settlements. Only some operate as collectivities now. They will have to reconstruct themselves as nations.

We believe strongly that membership in Aboriginal nations should *not* be defined by race. Aboriginal nations are political communities, often comprising people of mixed background and heritage. Their bonds are those of culture and identity, not blood. Their unity comes from their shared history and their strong sense of themselves as peoples.

The work of reconstructing their nations poses great challenges for Aboriginal people. They will need to

■ reconnect communities split apart by years of band or settlement administration

■ develop constitutions, design structures, and train personnel to make laws and administer decisions

■ negotiate new relations with the other two orders of government in Canada

They will need to develop their human resources. They will have to build an Aboriginal public service from the strong base in community administration they have now. They will have to encourage the attitudes necessary to be self-governing. And they will have to promote healing – the deep social and spiritual recovery process already under way in many Aboriginal communities.

To support the rebuilding of Aboriginal nations and shift from paternalistic policies to partnership relations, we propose a bold starting place: a new Royal Proclamation, issued by the Monarch as Canada's head of state and guardian of the rights of Aboriginal peoples.

A new proclamation would signal, in dramatic terms, a new day for Aboriginal people. Its all-important preamble should contain these elements:

■ Reaffirmation of Canada's respect for Aboriginal peoples as distinct nations.

- Acknowledgement of harmful actions by past governments, which deprived Aboriginal peoples of their lands and resources and interfered with family life, spiritual practices and governance structures.
- A statement placing the relationship on a footing of respect, recognition, sharing and mutual responsibility – thus ending the cycle of blame and guilt and freeing Aboriginal and non-Aboriginal people to embrace a shared future.
- Affirmation of the right of Aboriginal peoples to fashion their own lives and control their own governments and lands – not as a grant from other Canadian governments, but as a right inherent in them as peoples who have occupied these lands from time immemorial.
- Acknowledgement that justice and fair play are essential for reconciliation between Aboriginal and non-Aboriginal people and a commitment by Canada to create institutions and processes to strive for justice.

The proclamation should be followed by the enactment of companion legislation by the Parliament of Canada – legislation to create the new laws and institutions needed to implement the renewed relationship. Their combined purpose is to provide the authority and tools for Aboriginal people to structure their own political, social and economic future.

Of particular importance among these laws is an Aboriginal Nations Recognition and Government Act to give the government of Canada a mechanism for acknowledging established Aboriginal nations once their processes of internal reconstruction and institution building are complete.

To prepare for the new start, the federal government will need to undergo some reorganization of its own:

- The Department of Indian Affairs and Northern Development and the ministerial position that goes with it should be eliminated.
- A new senior cabinet position, the Minister for Aboriginal Relations, and a new Department of Aboriginal Relations should be assigned to negotiate and manage new

Traditionally, there were checks and balances that were functional and appropriate for the Anishnabek. The leaders were servants to the people and upheld the values that were inherent in the community. Accountability was not a goal or aim of the system; rather it was embedded in the very make-up of the system.

Union of Ontario Indians Brief to the Commission (1993)

agreements and arrangements from the federal government's side.

■ Another minister, the Minister of Indian and Inuit Services, and a new Indian and Inuit Services department should be assigned to deliver the gradually diminishing services coming from the federal level.

The Prime Minister should assume responsibility for launching and sustaining the renewed relationship and signal the significance of the new deal by participating at every stage.

MODELS AND POWERS OF SELF-GOVERNMENT

Aboriginal visions of self-government are as varied as their traditions, circumstances and aspirations. Scores of detailed proposals for self-government have been drawn up by Aboriginal peoples across Canada. The Commission identified three basic models, each with many possible variations. These models are all realistic and workable in the framework of the Canadian federation.

Nation Government

Aboriginal people with a strong sense of shared identity and an exclusive territorial base will probably opt for the 'nation' model of self-government. Inside their boundaries, nation governments would exercise a wide range of powers and authority. They might choose to incorporate elements of traditional governance. They could choose a loose federation among regions or communities, or a more centralized form of government. They will need to find ways of representing the interests of non-Aboriginal residents in decision making.

Public Government

In some regions, Aboriginal people are the majority in territory they share with non-Aboriginal people – for example, in the more northerly parts of the country. Existing agreements (such as the Nunavut Agreement) signal that Aboriginal nations in that situation will probably opt for the 'public' model of self-government. In this model, all residents participate equally in the functions of government, regardless of their heritage. Structures and processes of government would likely be similar to those of other Canadian governments – but with adaptations to reflect Aboriginal traditions and protect Aboriginal cultures.

Community of Interest Government

In urban centres, Aboriginal people from many nations form a minority of the population. They are not 'nations' in the way we define it, but they want a measure of self-government nevertheless – especially in relation to education, health care, economic development, and protection of their cultures. Urban Aboriginal governments could operate effectively within municipal boundaries, with voluntary membership and powers delegated from Aboriginal nation governments and/or provincial governments.

In our judgement, the right of Aboriginal governments to exercise authority over all matters relating to the good government and welfare of Aboriginal peoples and their territories is an existing Aboriginal right and is therefore recognized and affirmed by the constitution.

This governing authority has two parts: a

THE TESLIN TLINGIT NATION in the Yukon are building from the clan to the nation through the establishment of several branches of government: a general council, an executive council, an elders council and a justice council. While these councils are not duplicates of traditional Tlingit institutions, they do reflect the importance of the clans in their composition and in their consensual decision-making style.

CORE ABORIGINAL JURISDICTION

Core areas of Aboriginal jurisdiction are likely to include

- citizenship and membership
- government institutions
- elections and referendums
- access to and residence in the territory
- lands, waters, sea-ice and natural resources
- protection and management of the environment
- economic life, including commerce, labour, agriculture, hunting, trapping, fishing, etc.
- regulation of businesses, trades and professions
- management of public monies and other assets
- taxation
- family matters, including marriage, divorce, adoption and child custody
- property rights, including succession and estates
- health
- social welfare, including child welfare
- education
- language, culture, values and traditions
- some aspects of criminal law and procedure
- administration of justice
- policing
- housing and public works

'core' and a 'periphery'. The core of Aboriginal jurisdiction consists of matters that are of vital concern to the life and welfare of a particular Aboriginal people, its culture and identity – but do not have a major impact on neighbouring communities and are not otherwise the object of transcendant federal or provincial interest.

Legally, nothing prevents Aboriginal governments from taking charge of core issues in their communities and nations tomorrow. Practically, of course, they are tied into existing program arrangements with other governments. Before they can reasonably be expected to take charge, agreements about new funding formulas and many other issues are needed.

Matters on the periphery of Aboriginal jurisdiction – matters that affect the lands, resources and other interests of neighbouring people – must be subject to agreements with other governments. We have in mind such occasionally controversial issues as pollution control, road and rail access, wildlife protection, certain aspects of the justice system and so on – issues that will require shared or co-operative management arrangements.

FINANCING FOR SELF-GOVERNMENT

The financing of Aboriginal governments will require new approaches – approaches that acknowledge that much of the wealth of this country comes from lands and resources to which, in many cases, Aboriginal people have a legitimate claim.

If self-government is accompanied by fair redistribution of lands and resources – as we argue it must be – Aboriginal governments can become largely self-financing in the long term through greater access to what are called 'own-source revenues'. Own-source revenues flow to governments through familiar channels – taxation, investment, borrowing, business fees and royalties, public corporation revenues, proceeds from lotteries and gaming, and so on. These sources of revenue can and should be made available to Aboriginal governments.

It is especially important for Aboriginal governments to develop their own taxation systems. Most Aboriginal people pay taxes now, but to

provincial and federal governments. We are recommending that those who live on Aboriginal nation territories pay taxes primarily to their own governments. Those who live off Aboriginal territory would continue to pay taxes to federal and provincial governments.

It will take time for Aboriginal nations to develop own-source revenues. Even then, transfer payments from other governments will be needed – but to a lesser extent. We expect that treaties and other agreements among governments will free transfer payments from some of the restrictions on their use that now frustrate Aboriginal people.

Aboriginal nations, like the provinces, will have unequal access to resources and economic opportunities, so their level of prosperity will vary. We expect that nations that are well-off will help those that are not. Transfer payments from other governments will help to equalize the levels of service they can provide.

We also expect that, as they develop, Aboriginal nations will use their resources to take fiscal responsibility for their own governments and services. Transfer payments can be structured to encourage this, as now happens between the federal and provincial governments.

In the old days, we had a tradition of caring and sharing. If a man was sick or injured, the chief would delegate others to hunt for him and provide fire wood [for his family]. We redistributed our wealth for the good of all. And that is just what any good system of taxation is supposed to do.
Elder Ernie Crowe
quoted by
Chief Clarence Jules
Kamloops First Nation
community

REDISTRIBUTING LANDS AND RESOURCES

All over the world and throughout history, collective control of lands and resources has been the key to prosperity and the basis of the powerful idea of 'home' that gives a people their common identity. Most Aboriginal people retain an intensely spiritual connection to the land of their ancestors – one that involves both continuity and stewardship. It is hardly surprising, then, that the most intense conflicts between Aboriginal and non-Aboriginal people centre on the use and control of land.

Across Canada, Aboriginal people are pressing for an expanded share – a fair share – of lands and resources that were once theirs alone. They were promised as much by the Crown of England and its successor, the government of Canada. Some Aboriginal nations signed treaties only because of that promise.

In fact, though, except in northern Quebec and the territories, the amount of land allocated for use by Aboriginal people is extremely small. Aboriginal lands south of the 60th parallel (mainly Indian reserves) make up less than one-half of one per cent of the Canadian land mass. By contrast, in the United States (excluding Alaska), where Aboriginal people make up a far smaller portion of the population, they hold three per cent of the land (see map).

Land reserved for Aboriginal people was steadily whittled away after its original allocation. Almost two-thirds of it has 'disappeared' by various means since Confederation. In some cases, the government failed to deliver as much land as specified in a treaty. In other cases, it expropriated or sold reserved land, rarely with First Nations as willing vendors. Once in a while, outright fraud took place. Even when First Nations were able to keep hold of reserved land, the government sometimes sold its resources to outsiders.

These disappearances took place despite the solemn duty of the Crown to manage lands and resources for the benefit of Aboriginal people.

Similarly, Métis people, who believed they had won the right to their own lands and resources in the bargain with Ottawa that led to

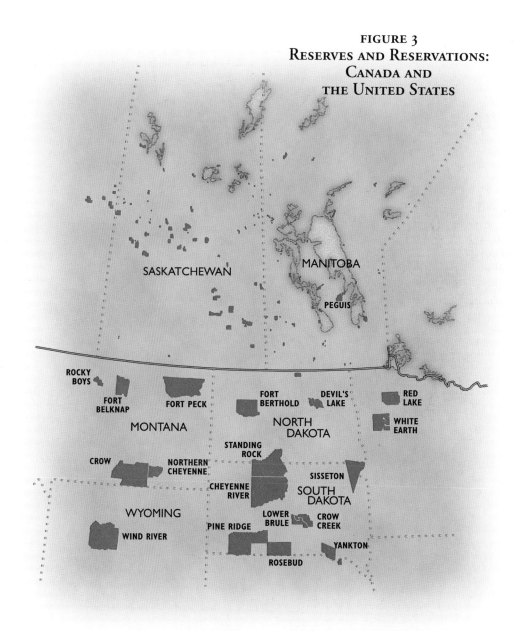

FIGURE 3
RESERVES AND RESERVATIONS:
CANADA AND
THE UNITED STATES

Source: Adapted, with permission, from Robert White-Harvey, "Reservation Geography and Restoration of Native Self-Government", *Dalhousie Law Journal* 17/2 (Fall 1994), p. 588.

the *Manitoba Act*, were driven further and further west – and ultimately dispersed as a people – by the largely fraudulent manner in which that bargain was administered.

Several other land policy issues have festered over the years:

■ Governments have failed to allocate any lands at all to some Aboriginal nations.
■ Governments have refused (with a few exceptions) to extend the land and resource base of First Nations as their populations, and their need for economic opportunity, grew.
■ Large-scale resource development projects have had a destructive impact on Aboriginal lands and communities.
■ Aboriginal peoples' treaty-protected harvesting rights on traditional lands have been opposed and blocked by non-Aboriginal people and governments.

Early in the relationship, colonial governments respected Aboriginal land rights and title. But over time, conflict grew. To non-Aboriginal people and governments, the many millions of unfarmed, undeveloped hectares of Canada were 'Crown land', public land – *their* land. To Aboriginal people, land belonged only to the Creator, but by virtue of their role as stewards, it was theirs to care for, to use – and to share if they chose.

Treaty agreements did not end the conflict. Indeed, it became sharper as settlers took up residence next door to Aboriginal people, who had not foreseen how deeply settlers' ways would clash with their own. They thought that the Crown's treaty promises would be enough to ensure their survival and independence. They were wrong.

The conflict became more deeply entrenched when the *Constitution Act, 1867* – drafted without discussion with Aboriginal people – assigned legal ownership of all Crown lands to the provinces.

If what Aboriginal peoples thought they had won had been delivered – a reasonable share of lands and resources for their exclusive use, protection for their traditional economic activities, resource revenues from shared lands, and support for their participation in the new economy being shaped by the settlers – the position of Aboriginal

We find ourselves without any real home in this, our own country... Our people are fined and imprisoned for...using the same game and fish which we were told would always be ours for food. Gradually we are becoming regarded as trespassers over a large portion of this, our country.
Chiefs of the Shuswap Okanagan and Couteau (Thompson) Tribes of British Columbia
Letter to Prime Minister Sir Wilfrid Laurier (1910)

peoples in Canada today would be very different. They would be major land owners. Most Aboriginal nations would likely be economically self-reliant. Some would be prosperous.

Some Aboriginal nations have gone to court to force governments to recognize their rights to land and resources, and some have been successful. A series of court decisions has confirmed that Aboriginal peoples have more than a strong moral case for redress on land and resource issues – they have legal rights.

The law of Aboriginal title establishes three things:

- Aboriginal people have rights of occupancy or use of portions of Canada that far exceed their current land base. These rights are based on their history of having lived in and used those lands since time immemorial.
- Agreements between the Crown and an Aboriginal nation (such as treaties) must be worked out before non-Aboriginal people can occupy or use that nation's traditional lands.
- The Crown of Canada is the guardian of Aboriginal title to their traditional lands and is obliged to support and protect their interests in those lands.

But the courts are a cumbersome, costly and sometimes insensitive way to solve the human

issues that underlie land and resource claims. Negotiated settlements, in which the parties talk face to face and work out complex deals, are preferable. Indeed, in nation-to-nation relations, they are essential.

Lands and resources are owing to Aboriginal peoples for both contemporary and historical reasons. Lands and resources are the essential sub-

structure of political, economic and social development. To rebuild their nations, Aboriginal people need

- enough land to give them something to call
  'home' – not just a physical space but a place
  of cultural and spiritual meaning as well
- enough land to allow for traditional pursuits,
  such as hunting and trapping
- enough lands and resources for economic
  self-reliance
- enough lands and resources to contribute significantly to the financing of self-government

FAIR SHARING: A PLAN

For many years, Canada has had a land claims
process. Its purpose is to allow First Nations to
pursue either a specific claim – for example, the
return of reserve land improperly sold off by the
government – or a comprehensive claim to an
allotment of the nation's traditional land in a case
where it has no treaty or other settlement with
Canada.

The existing land claims settlement process is
deeply flawed:

- It assumes that no Aboriginal rights apply on
  Crown land – unless Aboriginal nations can
  prove otherwise. This position is at odds
  with the doctrine of continuing Aboriginal
  title and with the duty of the Crown to protect Aboriginal interests.
- The government of Canada controls the
  process. It acts as defender of the Crown's
  interests and also as judge and jury on claims.
  This is a clear conflict of interest, since it con-
  siders itself the 'loser' when a claim is settled
  in favour of Aboriginal people.
- The process is not generally open to Métis
  claims, leaving Métis people without a land

and resource base and with no way of settling their grievances.

■ The government has always (except in one instance) required Aboriginal claimants to give up – or 'extinguish' – their general Aboriginal land rights, in favour of specific terms laid down in the settlement. Aboriginal people cannot accept the rupture of their special relationship with their lands that extinguishment implies.

A new process for negotiating the fair distribution of lands and resources is long overdue. The Commission proposes that this be handled as part of a new treaty process (outlined later in the chapter). The process would result in three categories of land allocation:

1. Lands selected from traditional territories that would belong exclusively to Aboriginal nations and be under their sole control.

2. Other lands in their traditional territories that would belong jointly to Aboriginal and non-Aboriginal governments and be the object of shared management arrangements.

3. Land that would belong to and remain under the control of the Crown but to which Aboriginal people would have special rights, such as a right of access to sacred and historical sites.

The third one would be the largest category of lands.

As a support to the new process, we are recommending establishment of regional treaty commissions and an Aboriginal Lands and Treaties Tribunal.

Regional treaty commissions would facilitate and support treaty negotiations but would not conduct negotiations – this would remain the responsibility of political leaders.

The tribunal would be responsible, first and foremost, for ensuring that treaty negotiations were carried out in good faith and financed fairly. Second, it would ensure that the interests of all parties were protected while treaties were being negotiated. Third, it would rule on discrete, specific claims that are capable of settlement in the short term.

The new treaty processes we propose will take

We believe the principle of sharing of our homeland [and] its natural resources is the basis of the treaty arrangements… Accordingly, the concepts of resource co-management and revenue sharing from the Crown lands are the proper forms of treaty implementation.

Chief George Fern
Prince Albert Tribal Council
La Ronge, Saskatchewan

In 1988, the Meadow Lake Tribal Council (MLTC) of northwestern Saskatchewan got help from the federal government to buy a 40 per cent share in a struggling pulp mill, NorSask Forest Products, and update the mill's equipment. Help from the provincial government produced a tree-farm licence. The MLTC then launched new businesses to do reforestation, logging and road construction. MLTC businesses have since paid $11 million in taxes and saved $10 million in social assistance costs by employing 240 people who would otherwise have been jobless.

time to show results. Steps must be taken in the meantime to provide enough lands and resources to meet Aboriginal nations' immediate needs.

■ The federal government can help First Nations add to their existing land base by (1) allocating all land promised to them in existing treaties; (2) returning to First Nations all land it has expropriated or bought, then left unused; and (3) establishing a fund to help Aboriginal people purchase land on the open market.

■ Aboriginal people have been largely excluded from the resource industries of Canada – even forestry and fisheries, where they once played a significant part in the labour force. Governments can revise their policies and set up programs to increase access to natural resources for Aboriginal people.

■ Governments can continue along the route toward co-management arrangements with Aboriginal people. The goal of co-management is shared responsibility for and benefits from particular resources where overlapping interests are great, such as fisheries on the

west coast, forestry in many regions, and all resources in certain national and provincial parks.

Failure to redistribute land and resources will doom Aboriginal people to a state of dependency on other Canadians – a sure recipe for grievance on both sides.

ECONOMIC DEVELOPMENT

Aboriginal people want to make a decent living, to be free of dependence on others, free of the social stigma and sense of personal failure that go with dependence, and free of the debilitating effects of poverty. Economic self-reliance will let them thrive as individuals and as nations and make their new governments a success.

The historical self-sufficiency of Aboriginal people and nations was destroyed in several ways:

■ Their control over their lands and resources was diminished or usurped.
■ New forms of economic activity (agriculture, manufacturing) were monopolized by non-Aboriginal people and businesses.
■ Governments failed to live up to the spirit

and intent of treaty promises to preserve traditional means of self-sufficiency – hunting, fishing, trapping, trading – and to help Aboriginal people take up the trades and occupations of the settlers if they wished.

■ Legislation, especially the *Indian Act*, interfered with economic activity on reserves by restricting the flow of capital and limiting the decision-making capacity of First Nations governments and entrepreneurs.

■ Businesses, industries and other workplaces have begun only recently and occasionally to welcome and accommodate Aboriginal people as employees.

■ Education and training facilities have begun only recently and occasionally to support Aboriginal people as students, with the result that few adults are equipped to compete for good jobs.

Several factors will make revitalization of Aboriginal economies a big challenge:

■ **Dependence**: Most Aboriginal nations and communities are highly dependent on funds from other governments. Most offer only a

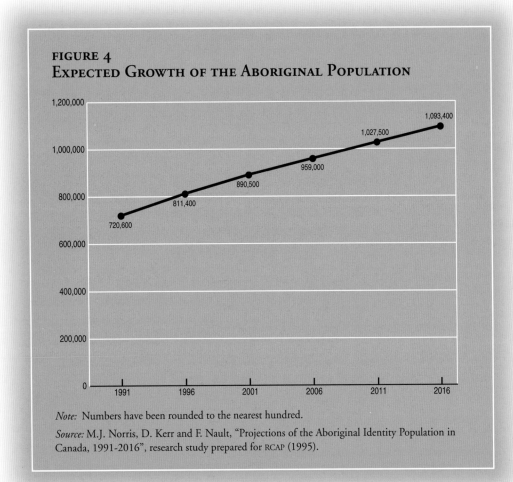

FIGURE 4
EXPECTED GROWTH OF THE ABORIGINAL POPULATION

Note: Numbers have been rounded to the nearest hundred.

Source: M.J. Norris, D. Kerr and F. Nault, "Projections of the Aboriginal Identity Population in Canada, 1991-2016", research study prepared for RCAP (1995).

limited range of job opportunities. Few can hold out the promise of jobs for the majority of their children.

■ **Inequality:** In 1991, 54 per cent of Aboriginal people had annual incomes of less than $10,000, as compared to 34 per cent of Canadians generally. Unemployment is high, and it has risen noticeably in the last decade as the size of the youth population has swelled.

■ **Rapid labour force growth:** Higher birth rates and life expectancy have produced a sharp increase in the Aboriginal population (see graph). The number of children under 16 is especially high, with sobering implications for future job needs.

■ **Variability:** Aboriginal nations are located all over the country, from east to west and north to south, from isolated villages to urban enclaves. Most have limited natural resources at their command, although many have riches under their feet. Economic activity in communities ranges from traditional harvesting to modern wage work. Economies may be restricted by the *Indian Act*, assisted by federal programs – or outside the reach of both.

Because of this complexity, means and strategies to achieve self-reliance will vary. No single economic development plan or program will work.

Ownership of lands and resources is essential to create income and wealth for Aboriginal individuals and nations. But ownership is not enough. Communities and nations that want to control the wealth available from their resources don't want to leave operation of their economies to outside specialists. The challenge of skills development to meet the demands of both modern and traditional economic activity is just beginning to be met in Aboriginal communities.

Federal, provincial and territorial governments should co-operate to stimulate economic vitality in both the traditional and the modern sector – so that all Aboriginal people have the chance to make a reasonable living, whether as a carver in Cape Dorset, a teacher in Saskatoon, or a part-time trapper and radio technician in Moose Factory.

Recent progress in economic development gives rise to hope for a brighter future. But the challenge of turning pockets of progress into a broad transformation of economic life for Aboriginal people remains immense.

LEVERS OF ECONOMIC CHANGE

Transforming Aboriginal economies from dependence to self-reliance will not be easy. The greatest boost for most nations will come from access to a fair share of lands and resources.

The results of recent land claims settlements suggest that nations will use their timber, minerals, fish, wildlife and other resources to create jobs, bring in revenue, and lay the foundation of a diversified economy. Access to resources is the key, but increasing the land and resource base is not enough. Other strategies are needed too.

Regaining Control

As things stand, Aboriginal communities are subject to a changing array of economic development programs, most of them managed from

THERE ARE ONLY FIVE registered professional foresters and fewer than ten registered professional geologists of Aboriginal ancestry in all of Canada.

IN A RECENT DISCUSSION PAPER on social security reform, Human Resources Development Canada estimated that 45 per cent of all new jobs created between 1990 and 2000 will require more than 16 years of education and training.

THE QUEBEC CREE of eastern James Bay signed the 1975 James Bay and Northern Quebec Agreement, a modern treaty. The Ontario Cree of western James Bay signed Treaty 9 in 1905-06. The former have improved their economic status. The eastern Cree have more land, more access to resources and more capital than their western neighbours. Although the eastern Cree have disputes with Quebec about the full extent of their rights, the western Cree would love to have their problems. The western Cree have only limited access to land and resources and no money for such creative initiatives as the eastern Cree's income security program for traditional harvesters.

distant government offices. They must tailor their ideas for stimulating the economy to program criteria set by external authorities.

We call on federal and provincial governments to enter into long-term development agreements with Aboriginal nations to provide support, advice and stable funding for economic development. Aboriginal nations would design programs, make investment decisions, and be accountable to their people for managing these resources.

Regaining control of economic matters without the human resources and capacity to manage them would spell trouble for Aboriginal nations. They must be helped to develop the personnel and the regional and national institutions they need to invest in and manage businesses in specific sectors – resource extraction industries, agriculture, communications, tourism, and so on.

Business Development

Governments have worked with Aboriginal entrepreneurs to help make business development one of the sparks of economic growth in Aboriginal communities. Many have demonstrated their capacity to master a wide range of commercial skills as individual entrepreneurs and as managers of community-owned businesses.

■ Levels of business formation have been high

in recent years. About 10 per cent of Aboriginal people report business ownership or income from self-employment.

■ Self-employment has increased markedly in the last decade, particularly among Aboriginal women.

Entrepreneurs face the same challenges everywhere: the need to plan, raise money, produce a good product and market it effectively. But Aboriginal entrepreneurs face other obstacles too: limited capital for investment, distrust from banks and other financial institutions, absence of local business services and advisers, tiny local markets, and sometimes even hostility at home and from nearby communities.

Aboriginal nations have had perhaps their greatest successes through collectively owned enterprises – where shares in the company are held by the community or the nation government on behalf of its members. Through their companies, communities run regional airlines. They are involved in forestry management, silviculture, wood harvesting and processing. They run grocery stores and wholesale food distribut-

ing networks, motels, hotels, bowling alleys, golf courses and much more.

Some have had a rough ride – making mistakes, losing investments, sometimes experiencing bankruptcy. But valuable lessons have been learned, and there are now scores of Aboriginal people with the skills and confidence to manage the operations of modern commercial enterprises.

They, and those who would follow in their footsteps, still need support. We recommend that Aboriginal and non-Aboriginal governments work together to develop

■ improved business services
■ improved access to loan and equity capital, including the creation of a national Aboriginal development bank
■ improved access to markets

Employment

The employment problem is immense. More than 80,000 jobs are needed now, just to raise Aboriginal people's employment rate to the over-

My father-in-law, when he first heard that welfare was to be introduced in the North, shuddered at this solution, [saying that] it will not create a long-term economic solution that is acceptable to Inuit, but it will create a great dependency, where no one will ever get out.
Charlie Evalik
Cambridge Bay,
Northwest Territories

RON JAMIESON, A MOHAWK from the Six Nations and a vice-president of the Bank of Montreal: "There is a perception in the Aboriginal and non-Aboriginal communities that Aboriginal people lack the skills and temperament to be effective entrepreneurs. I challenge that assumption." Jamieson identified four qualities essential for modern business that have long characterized Aboriginal people: risk taking, discipline, clarity of vision, and ability to meet the needs of the community or client.

all Canadian rate. Without action, the situation will deteriorate. The Aboriginal population is young: 56 per cent are under 24 years of age, compared with 34 per cent of all Canadians. An additional 225,000 jobs will have to be found in the next 20 years to put them to work.

We propose a sustained effort to increase employment for Aboriginal people, including

- a special 10-year program to train Aboriginal people for the work that has to be done in newly self-governing nations
- a new approach to employment equity, in which employers work with Aboriginal organizations to forecast vacancies and train Aboriginal people to fill them
- measures to increase the number of Aboriginal employment service agencies and their capacity to place Aboriginal people in the labour force
- provision of culturally appropriate and affordable child care, so that more Aboriginal parents can join the labour force

Education and Training

Public investment in education and training is vital to improve employment prospects for Aboriginal people in the existing job market. There are shortages of trained Aboriginal people in such fields as economics, medicine, engineering, community planning, forestry, wildlife management, geology and agriculture – to name only a few.

Aboriginal nations cannot rebuild their political institutions, manage their economies or staff their social services without trained people. Yet high school and university completion rates are low among Aboriginal youth.

Motivating youth to complete their education is of great importance to the economic future of Aboriginal communities. Youth need a strong foundation in their traditions and proficiency in the skills valued by contemporary society. Those who master these skills and contribute to their communities and nations deserve to be celebrated as the modern equivalents of the great hunters and leaders of the past.

Education and training are discussed in more detail in Chapter 3.

Alternatives to Welfare

The need for welfare in Aboriginal communities came with the confiscation of ever expanding tracts of their land. Indigenous people grew poor, malnourished and sick. Many died young. The government chose to provide short-term 'relief' instead of sustained help to rebuild ravaged Aboriginal economies – a choice governments have made over and over again in the last two centuries.

By the 1960s, welfare had become available to Aboriginal people as it was to other Canadians. Since then, more and more have become dependent. The rate of welfare dependence is now two to four times higher among Aboriginal people than among Canadians generally. Many speakers at the Commission's public hearings lamented the erosion of self-reliance among peoples once renowned for it, an erosion brought about by the combination of economic ruin and welfare availability.

There may never be enough jobs to go around in Aboriginal communities. Yet social assistance, as now delivered, is not a good way of

SOME YEARS AGO, in the Dene community of Fort Franklin in the Northwest Territories, the council decided to use a portion of welfare funds to pay welfare recipients to do much needed work around town: remodelling and repainting public buildings, cleaning public spaces, gathering wood for elders and single mothers. Although these projects had some success in meeting their goals, they were stopped by the funding government when authorities found out that recipients were working for welfare.

providing cash income, for it traps recipients in a marginal existence. It may protect against abject poverty, but it can also stifle individual initiative, and it does little to deal with the community conditions that lead to dependence.

We think Aboriginal communities should be able to use the money now earmarked for individual welfare payments as an instrument of broader economic development:

■ Aboriginal communities or nations could take charge of the funds their residents now receive for social assistance. These funds, along with a top-up amount for capital and other costs, could be used for local projects such as new roads, a community centre or a business venture. The able-bodied unemployed could work on these projects, receiving wages rather than welfare. They would gain experience and skills, and the community as a whole would benefit from their work.

■ The maze of assistance programs available in urban centres could be simplified through single-window service delivery. Funds now available for life skills, job training, job finding, child care and income maintenance could be pooled to support holistic planning to help individuals make changes in their lives.

■ In remote areas, income support funds could be used to support hard-to-finance activities such as traditional harvesting. The James Bay Cree Income Security Program provides a model.

These reforms are urgent. Commission research predicts that, unless economic conditions and welfare programs on reserves change radically and soon, the bill for social assistance will reach $1 billion by 1999 and $1.5 billion by 2002.

TREATIES: THE MECHANISM OF CHANGE

The Commission proposes a wide-ranging agenda for change to achieve two goals:

■ Rebuilding Aboriginal nations as the best and proper way for Aboriginal people to protect their heritage and identity, restore health and prosperity to their communities, and reorganize their relations with Canada.

■ Restoration of relations of mutual respect and fair dealing between Aboriginal and non-Aboriginal people.

As complex as the project appears, *it can be done.* The central mechanism of change is the treaty.

Treaties have a long and honourable history as a way of solving disputes between peoples, nations and governments. Although Canada's historical treaties with Aboriginal nations have been ignored and violated over the years, the treaty format is still a powerful way of stating the terms of a relationship.

To see how treaties can be used in the modern context, Canadians need to understand them better. In brief, the historical treaties are

■ **Promises exchanged between the governments of France, Britain and Canada, and Aboriginal peoples.**
To secure peace or alliance with Aboriginal nations, or gain occupancy and development rights on Aboriginal land, the Crowns of France, Britain and, later, Canada promised Aboriginal peoples protection, benefits and shares of wealth – in perpetuity. Those promises now rest with the governments of Canada.

■ **Nation-to-nation agreements.**
Treaties are not admissions of defeat or submission. Parties to a treaty do not give up nationhood or their own ways of living, working and governing themselves. Rather, they acknowledge their shared wish to live in peace and harmony, agree on rules of coexistence, then work to fulfil their commitments to one another.

■ **Commitments that are sacred and enduring.**
The historical treaties were taken very seriously by both sides. Their purpose was to create a relationship of peace and friendship that would last. The alternative was lost trade and possibly warfare and bloodshed. Treaties were sworn by sacred oaths, announced with great ceremony, and regarded as binding documents of state. The fact that they have been violated time and again does not change their underlying legitimacy.

■ **Part of Canada's constitution.**
The treaties set out broad social contracts between independent peoples, very like the terms

Treaties have a long and honourable history as a way of solving disputes between peoples, nations and governments.

of union by which former British colonies joined
Confederation as provinces. They are constitutional documents, recognized and affirmed in
section 35 of the *Constitution Act, 1982.* As such,
they are part of the law of the land.

■ **Fundamental to Canada's honour.**
Treaty making is one of the great achievements of
human societies. It enables the deepest conflicts
to be set aside in favour of respectful coexistence.
It expresses the choice to live in harmony with
others, rather than spill blood or exercise power
using more subtle forms of violence. The act of
entering into a treaty, then as now, represents a
profound commitment between peoples. Once
made, a treaty is broken or ignored only at the
cost of a stain on the good name of the nation or
government that breaks it.

We propose that the treaty relationship be
restored and used from now on as the basis of the
partnership between Aboriginal and non-
Aboriginal people in Canada.

This will require the fulfilment and renewal
of existing treaties and the making of new treaties
with Aboriginal peoples who do not have them
now.

Treaty Fulfilment and Renewal

Accounts of negotiations leading to the historical
treaties are full of stories of miscommunication
and cross purposes. This is hardly surprising.
Negotiators had no common language, no common frame of reference. Despite profoundly different cultures and world views, they were trying
to figure out how to share a world.

Implementation of treaty terms and promises
was problematic from the start. As time passed
and the balance of power between Aboriginal and
non-Aboriginal people shifted, governments were
able to ignore terms and promises that no longer
suited them. For example,

■ The Anishnabe (Ojibwa) of Lake Huron and
Lake Superior were promised that the annu-
ity money they received for use of their traditional lands would increase if the revenues
derived from their resources increased.
■ The people of the Okanagan Valley in British
Columbia were promised that if they opened
their valley to settlers, they could choose
reserve lands of any size and location.

■ The chiefs of northwestern Ontario were promised the right to hunt and fish on Crown land forever, if they signed Treaty 9.

These promises were not honoured. Canadians believe in fair dealing, and treaty fulfilment, even after all these years, is still an imperative for Canada.

Treaty renewal is a way of addressing fundamental disagreements between Aboriginal and non-Aboriginal authorities about the accuracy of the treaties and about their real purpose.

Many Aboriginal people say that the written version of treaties fails to reflect crucial verbal agreements reached by negotiators. Further, they say that the treaties are not just records of a deal, but attempts to give shape to the infinitely complex business of sharing a country. They are agreements for living together and thus are living agreements that must be reviewed and reinterpreted periodically in light of their purpose – their 'spirit and intent'.

Non-Aboriginal governments take a much more restrictive view. They argue that the written

treaty is the complete treaty and that it should be interpreted literally.

The historical evidence is clear on the first point of disagreement: the written treaties often are *not* a full and fair statement of agreements reached.

On the second point, the Commission has concluded that *the treaties should be implemented to reflect their spirit and intent* – not just their words, whether spoken or written. The language of yesterday's treaties reflects yesterday's values.

For example, the $5 annual treaty money – a gift commemorating the agreement in Aboriginal eyes, a form of rent for use of the land in European eyes – was a significant sum in its time. Or, to take another example, the promise of a medicine chest for those who signed Treaty 6 was a commitment to provide the best health care available at that time.

It is deeply self-serving of Canadian authorities to insist on a literal interpretation of such clauses. If the relationship between Aboriginal and non-Aboriginal people is ever to be set right, the underlying intentions of treaty promises –

not the letter of outdated terms – must guide their present-day implementation.

To bring about fulfilment and renewal of the historical treaties, we recommend that Canadian governments

- honour the provisions of existing treaties as recorded in treaty text and supplemented by oral evidence
- interpret the terms of each treaty in a broad and liberal way, in keeping with the spirit and intent of the agreements reached
- act as protectors of Aboriginal interests, not adversaries, and reconcile the interests of society as a whole with the terms of the treaties
- recognize that First Nations did not consent to loss of title to their lands or to extinguish all rights to their lands when they signed treaties – a more reasonable interpretation is that they consented to share and co-manage lands and resources
- recognize that by entering into treaties with Aboriginal peoples, the Crown of Canada acknowledged their inherent right of self-government, their right to control their own

affairs, and their right to enter into intergovernmental arrangements with other nations

- establish a process for fulfilling and renewing existing treaties, on the basis of these principles

Making New Treaties

In the beginning, colonial and Canadian governments made treaties only with First Nations – and then, only some First Nations. In recent years, Canada has come to a few new treaty-like agreements, including those with

- Inuit and Crees (and later the Naskapi) of James Bay and Northern Quebec (1975 and 1978)
- Inuvialuit (and later Inuit) of the Northwest Territories (1984 and 1993)
- Yukon First Nations (1993)
- the Nisga'a in British Columbia (1996)

But many nations still have no treaty of any kind. We believe that those without a treaty, accord, compact or other agreement clarifying their relationship with Canada have the right to seek one.

For its part, Canada has a duty to conclude such treaties.

We propose a new treaty process to lead the way to reconciliation between Aboriginal and non-Aboriginal people over the next 20 years. An agreed treaty process can be the mechanism for implementing virtually all the recommendations in our report – indeed, it may be the only legitimate way to do so.

The main objectives of a new treaty-making process would be to

- establish the full jurisdiction of those nations as part of an Aboriginal order of government
- expand the land and resource base under their control

Canadians may ask why, after so many years of broken promises and dashed hopes, Aboriginal people would put any faith in a new process. We believe that their trust can be rekindled and their participation gained if the new treaty process is given a dramatic foundation in word and deed – in keeping with its stature as a tool of statecraft.

To set the stage, we recommend that Parliament declare its support for the treaty relationship in the form of a new Royal

It is self-defeating [for the government] to pursue a policy that supposes the terms of a claims agreement can be fixed for all time. There can be no acceptable final definition of the compromises that must be made between societies over succeeding generations. The conclusion of a modern claims agreement must be seen as a beginning, not an end.

Bernadette Makpah
Nunavut Tunngavik Inc.

Proclamation. By itself, a new proclamation will change nothing; it needs to be backed up by companion legislation setting out guiding principles for the treaty processes and establishing new decision-making bodies, independent of government, to conduct them.

One major piece of companion legislation would be an Aboriginal Treaties Implementation Act with the following provisions:

- It would establish a process for recognized Aboriginal nations to renew existing treaties or negotiate new ones.
- It would set out processes and principles to guide negotiation.
- Its guiding principles would include a commitment to implement existing treaties according to their spirit and intent and to renegotiate treaty terms on which there was no meeting of minds when they were originally set down.
- It would establish regional treaty commissions to convene and manage the negotiation process, with advice from the Aboriginal Lands and Treaties Tribunal on certain issues. To achieve legitimacy, treaty commissions would act at arm's length from government.

Their job would not be to determine the outcome of negotiations but to facilitate the process. Each treaty will be the result of a political agreement, freely entered into by all parties and agreed to by their constituencies.

Existing treaties can, should and must be fulfilled, and the treaty relationship should be extended to all Aboriginal nations. If done honestly and fairly, treaty making can restore the form and feeling of partnership in relations between Aboriginal and non-Aboriginal people.

Canada can afford to do this. Indeed, Canada cannot afford *not* to do it, for the cost of maintaining Aboriginal people in a state of dependence and social disorganization – measured in human distress, lost productivity and proliferating government programs – is enormous, as we show in Chapter 5.

The Relationship Restructured

In this chapter, we have outlined major steps needed to transform the relationship between Aboriginal people and other Canadians from its present state of tension and failed initiatives to one of co-operation and growing successes. The steps are numerous and may seem daunting. But they are logical, they are progressive, they reinforce each other, and they constitute a workable plan. Let us review them briefly:

1 **The federal government should begin the cycle of renewal with an act of national intention – a new Royal Proclamation.** The Commission is calling for a sharp break with past practices, mired as they are in fallacies about Aboriginal people and their rights, tarnished as they are with failed negotiations and broken promises. We propose a new Royal Proclamation, stating Canada's commitment to principles of mutual recognition, respect, responsibility and sharing in the relationship between original peoples and those who came later.

2 Parliament should enact companion legislation to give these intentions form and meaning and provide the legal instruments needed to implement them.

Three major pieces of legislation would be needed:

■ an Aboriginal Treaties Implementation Act, setting out a process for clarifying and modernizing existing treaties and making new ones, and establishing regional treaty commissions to facilitate and support the negotiation process

■ an Aboriginal Lands and Treaties Tribunal Act, establishing a body to clear the backlog of specific claims and act as ombudsman for the new comprehensive treaty-making processes

■ an Aboriginal Nations Recognition and Government Act, setting out the process and criteria for recognizing Aboriginal nations, acknowledging, on an interim basis (until treaty negotiations are complete), their jurisdiction over core issues within their existing territories, and providing financing

These steps should be undertaken in close consultation with national Aboriginal organizations and provincial and territorial governments. While consultations are under way, a public education campaign should be launched to promote understanding on the part of all Canadians.

3 **The federal government should provide a forum for negotiating a Canada-wide framework agreement to lay the ground rules for processes to establish the new relationship.**

The forum should be convened under the authority of the first ministers of federal, provincial and territorial governments and leaders of national Aboriginal organizations and should address at least these issues:

- treaty renewal and new treaty making
- redistribution of lands and resources
- clarification of areas of independent and shared jurisdiction
- redesign of short-term and long-term fiscal arrangements

4 **Aboriginal nations should begin their rebuilding processes.**

Aboriginal nations will need time and resources to undertake the nation building that must be completed before they seek formal recognition from Canada. In particular, they must clarify membership issues and develop institutions and human resources for self-government and all it entails.

5 **All governments should prepare to enter into the new treaty process.**

After recognition, each Aboriginal nation will need to seek a mandate from its citizens to enter into a treaty renewal or negotiation process. These negotiations will result in the settlement of land, resource, governance and financing issues.

The federal government will need legislation in place and reorganization of its internal structures, as we have recommended. The provinces will need parallel legislation permitting them to be partners in treaty processes within their boundaries.

Non-Indian governments...did not terminate the treaties. They did not restrict the treaties. They just forgot about the treaties, and our claim to the land...

Chief Albert Levi
Big Cove First Nation community
Big Cove, New Brunswick

6 Governments should take interim steps, as proposed by this Commission, to redistribute lands and resources.

Canada's wealth must be shared fairly with the original inhabitants of the land. Commitment to Aboriginal self-government will be hollow unless Aboriginal nations have access to an adequate land base, with resources to match. The greatest part of the decision making about redistribution will be done during treaty negotiations.

However, we have proposed interim measures to bring short-term relief, and we urge governments to pursue them.

7 Aboriginal and non-Aboriginal governments should co-operate to stimulate economic development.

Creating meaningful work for the citizens of Aboriginal nations will require long-term strategies to promote a mix of economic activity. The strategies we propose will require co-operation among governments, both before and after the broader processes of change are under way.

These steps, taken together, have the potential to bring about fundamental change – in the hearts, minds and life experience of Aboriginal people, who have waited so long for justice, and in Canada as a country of fair-minded people. Each step, and the rationale from which it springs, must be accepted and adopted with determination and good will, by Aboriginal and non-Aboriginal people and their leaders.

It can be done.

But it will not work unless Aboriginal people, in their nations and communities and personal lives, see that it does. To do so, they will need to develop and use their full potential as human beings and as citizens of their nations. This significant challenge is the subject of the next chapter.

I like to go hunting ducks.

gr 1

Darren

GATHERING STRENGTH

3

Aboriginal people endure ill health, run-down and overcrowded housing, polluted water, inadequate schools, poverty and family breakdown at rates found more often in developing countries than in Canada. These conditions are inherently unjust. They also imperil the future of Aboriginal communities and nations.

Many people who spoke to us urged us to consider the human problems facing Aboriginal people holistically – as part of a pattern of negative effects arising from their experience of life under policies of domination and assimilation. This approach helped us identify the key elements in solutions that will work.

■ Poverty, ill health, educational failure, family violence and other problems reinforce one another. To break the circle of disadvantage – where family violence leads to educational failure, which leads to poverty, which leads to ill health

and back to violence – all these conditions must be tackled together, not piecemeal.

■ Repeated assaults on the culture and collective identity of Aboriginal people (described in Chapter 1) have weakened the foundations of Aboriginal society and contributed to the alienation that drives some to self-destruction and anti-social behaviour. Social problems among Aboriginal people are, in large measure, a legacy of history.

■ Just as social problems spring in part from collective experience, so solutions require change at the collective level. Aboriginal people acting alone cannot shift the weight of disadvantage and discrimination. But solutions that lift the weight for Aboriginal people collectively shift it for everyone.

THE CIRCLE OF WELL-BEING

The elements in the Commission's agenda for fundamental change – self-government, economic self-reliance, a partnership of mutual respect with Canada, and healing in the broadest sense – form a circle of well-being that revolves something like this:

- Self-government will not succeed unless it has a solid foundation in economic activity and highly developed human skills.
- Aboriginal people will not regain the human capacities they need to rebuild their economies and communities unless they are self-governing.
- Once they are self-governing, self-reliant and healthy in body, mind and spirit, Aboriginal people will be able to take responsibility for themselves and their place in the partnership with Canada. The circle of well-being will be complete.

But pressing health and social problems cannot wait. As the wheels of change slowly turn,

Aboriginal children's lives are blighted by loss of culture, failure at school and violence at home. Teenagers are humiliated by racism and rejection by their peers. Whole communities suffer substandard housing, unclean water and other risks to health.

Canada's constitution makes room for Aboriginal people to take charge of these matters right now, if they want to – without waiting for other governments to transfer authority.

But agreements (treaties, accords, settlements) with other governments will ease the way forward, resolving tough political, administrative and financial issues in advance. Aboriginal communities will make more headway with health and social problems if they have the support and co-operation of other governments.

Treaty making takes time. The transition to full control of community affairs by Aboriginal people will take some years. Some will chafe at delay, but the passage of time has some advantages for Aboriginal people, for they are still gathering strength for the tasks ahead. They need

The process of healing must be based on our traditional spiritual values of respect, pride, dignity, sharing, hospitality and mutual aid... Self-reliance begins with the individual, then is built by the family, then by the community, and finally, by our relations with other nations.

Chief Jean-Charles Piétacho
and Sylvie Basile
Mingan First Nation
community

more trained people to meet the challenges of
self-government and new institutions to put the
stamp of aboriginality on social services and their
delivery.

As well, they need to work with non-
Aboriginal health and social services agencies to
transform relations with them. Mainstream services and agencies need to become more welcom-
ing and more sensitive to cultural difference. They
need to ensure that all traces of racism are eliminated from policy and practice. And they need to
start seeing Aboriginal people as partners in the
design, development and delivery of services.

Our recommendations on social and health
policy focus on three interlinked objectives:

- solving urgent health and social problems
- promoting human capacity building in
  Aboriginal nations
- alerting mainstream institutions to their
  responsibilities to Aboriginal people

Well-being flows from balance and harmony among all elements of personal and collective life.

THE CENTRALITY OF FAMILY

Many presenters at our public hearings argued that breakdown in traditional Aboriginal family structures and functions is a major factor in the social problems with which they are grappling. They argued for rehabilitation of Aboriginal families as part of the path to personal and community healing.

Family is still the central institution in Aboriginal societies. It is only a generation or two since extended kin networks of parents, grandparents and clan members made up virtually the entire social world for Aboriginal people, providing the framework for most of the business of life. Inside the web of family, norms of sharing and mutual aid provided a social safety net for every individual.

Aboriginal families, and the cultures and identities they passed on to their children, were severely disrupted by actions of colonial and Canadian governments. Children in particular were targeted time and again in official strategies to control and assimilate Aboriginal people.

■ **Residential schools** did the greatest damage. Children as young as 6 years old were removed from their families for 10 months of the year or longer. They were forbidden to speak the only languages they knew and taught to reject their homes, their heritage and, by extension, themselves. Most were subjected to physical deprivation, and some experienced abuse. We heard from a few people who are grateful for what they learned at these schools, but we heard from more who described deep scars – not least in their inability to give and receive love.

■ The removal of Aboriginal children from their communities through **cross-cultural foster placement and adoption** is a second major cause of family disruption. Children removed from their families are severed from their roots and grow up not knowing what it is to be Inuit, Métis or a First Nation member. Yet they are set apart from their new families and communities by visible difference and often made to feel ashamed of their origins. At the same time, their home communities and extended families are robbed of part of the next generation.

■ **Migration to cities and towns** also disrupts families. Aboriginal people leave home to improve their education, look for work or escape family violence. Once in the cities, they lose the family support they depended on at home. If they have troubles, they may find urban services difficult to penetrate, alien in spirit and perhaps racist. Many make a successful transition. But others fall into the cracks between cultures, where they are isolated, unemployed and under-served.

People who endure these disruptions may feel adrift – disoriented and unsure of how to get along in the sometimes hostile non-Aboriginal world. If their aboriginality has been devalued or ridiculed, they may have lost pride and self-esteem and be unable to build these qualities in their children. If they have been damaged in heart and soul, they may turn to alcohol, violence, crime or other forms of anti-social behaviour.

Many Aboriginal people told the Commission that the future they wish for – as self-governing, self-reliant nations within Canada – is impossible unless the strong bonds of family that gave individuals and communities their stability are rebuilt.

Services designed and controlled by Aboriginal people can do much to heal the wounds visible in statistics on social dysfunction – family breakdown, suicide and attempted suicide among youth, substance abuse, trouble with the law. To prevent them from recurring, the Aboriginal family must be restored to its traditional role as nurturer of the young and protector of the old, guardian of the culture and safety net for the vulnerable.

"Our Children Are Our Future"

Children have a special place in Aboriginal cultures. According to tradition, they are gifts from the spirit world and must be treated well or they will return to that realm.

Failure to protect a child from harm is perhaps the greatest shame that can befall an Aboriginal family. Yet it has happened repeatedly in the last several generations, and it continues to happen today.

Abuse and family violence are the most dramatic problems, but they are the tip of an iceberg that began to form when Aboriginal communities lost their independent self-determining powers

With the healing in place, we can have self-government. But without the healing, we will have dysfunctional self-government.
> Jeanette Costello
> Counsellor, Kitselas Drug and Alcohol Program
> Terrace, British Columbia

Most of our clients...are young, sole support mothers who were very often removed [from their families] as children themselves... And while the mother may have been in foster care, the grandmother – I think we all know where she was [as a child]. She was in residential school. So we are into a third generation [of disrupted families] now.
> Kenn Richard
> Executive Director, Native Child and Family Services
> Toronto, Ontario

Aboriginal children, was to tear more holes in the family web and detach more Aboriginal people from their roots.

Authorities had only one remedy for children thought to be in need of protection – removal from their families. Authorities were not able to alleviate family poverty, fix crumbling houses, or support young parents who had themselves been raised in institutions, without parents as models. They made little or no attempt to place children at risk with members of their kin network or with other Aboriginal families who could help them hold on to their culture and identity.

Child welfare is one of the services that Aboriginal people want most to control for themselves. In 1981, the federal government signed the first agreement authorizing a First Nations agency to deliver child welfare services. Since then, some three dozen Aboriginal agencies have been authorized. They have revised the rules of placement, to recognize the capacity of kin net-

and Aboriginal families were deprived of authority and influence over their children.

The source of social dysfunction we heard most about in public testimony was residential schooling, but inappropriate child welfare policies have also been a persistent and destructive force. The effect of these policies, as applied to

works to protect Aboriginal children, and emphasized the importance of cultural continuity in placements.

Even so, the well-being of the children is not assured. Aboriginal agencies have inherited many of the problems of the agencies they replaced. They struggle with ill-fitting rules made outside their communities; with levels of family distress and need beyond their limited resources; and with the challenge of finding ways to protect children at risk while respecting extended family networks that resist interference. Not all Aboriginal child welfare agencies have achieved the high standards to which they aspire.

Immediate action of three kinds is needed:

- **rehabilitation services** to promote healing and recovery for Aboriginal parents with serious problems
- **preventive services** to support Aboriginal families who are beginning to get into trouble
- **continued reform of existing services** – more local case evaluation and follow-up, more

appropriate training for personnel, more accessible and culturally appropriate urban services

The healthy functioning of Aboriginal families has been disrupted largely by misguided government policies. Today's governments have an obligation to make amends. In the next section we lay out our proposals for a thorough redesign of health and healing services, including child welfare. In the short term, we propose that

- all governments take action to increase and support Aboriginal control of child welfare services
- block funding replace per capita care allowances so that continuing preventive services can be developed
- more resources be made available for urban services

Ending the Cycle of Family Violence

Aboriginal people speaking at our public hearings, especially women, were frank about the extent and severe effects of family violence in Aboriginal life. They pointed to the need for

WHEN CAMERON KERLEY was 8 years old, he and his three sisters were taken into care by the Children's Aid Society and placed in foster homes. His mother died two years later of alcoholism. Cameron was then placed for adoption with Dick Kerley, an unmarried American man who had previously adopted another Indian boy. Cameron soon began to have problems, skipping school and getting into trouble with the law. When he was 19, he killed his adoptive father with a baseball bat. He pleaded guilty to second degree murder and was sentenced to a minimum of 15 years in prison. After sentencing, Cameron described sexual abuse by his adoptive father, beginning shortly after his placement. U.S. authorities would not reopen the case but allowed him to return to Manitoba to serve his sentence.

improved services, but they said that the best hope lies in restoration of traditional Aboriginal values of respect for women and children and reintegration of women into family, community and nation decision making.

The Canadian Panel on Violence Against Women (1993) stated that family violence arises from a fundamental imbalance of power between men and women. This is true for Aboriginal people, too, but this inequality exists within a greater imbalance of power – that between Aboriginal and non-Aboriginal society. In these circumstances, the loss, humiliation, frustration and anger shared by all Aboriginal people can provoke violence in some, as one speaker explained to us:

> The oppressed begin to develop what they call 'cultural self-shame' and 'cultural self-hate', which results in a lot of frustration and anger. At the same time...we begin to adopt our oppressors' values, and in a way, we become oppressors ourselves....We begin hurting our own people. When you talk about things like addiction and family abuse, elder abuse, sexual abuse, jealousy, gossip, suicide and all the different forms of abuse we seem to be experiencing, it's all based on [oppression].
>
> Roy Fabian, Executive Director
> Hay River Treatment Centre
> Hay River, Northwest Territories

Twenty-four per cent of the respondents to our questionnaire indicated that they know of deaths as a result of Aboriginal family violence, and 54 per cent...know of cases where a woman sustained injury which required medical treatment as a result of family violence but did not seek medical attention out of fear and shame.

Catherine Brooks
Director, Anduhyaun
Residence for Women
Toronto, Ontario

Family violence among Aboriginal people thus has its own dynamic, and public policy must take this into account.

- Violence and abuse are often part of a pattern of disrupted relationships, deadened feelings and weakened cultural rules for responsible behaviour, a pattern that can be traced back to government interventions.
- In some cases, a culture of violence has invaded communities. Incidents cannot be treated as the isolated problems of particular couples or households.
- Violence in Aboriginal communities is promoted and sustained by racist attitudes that perpetuate demeaning stereotypes, especially of Aboriginal women.

No matter where it occurs, family violence is hidden. Women hesitate to speak out for fear of triggering more abuse, or because they are ashamed and blame themselves for their situation. Aboriginal women stay silent for other reasons as well. They may fear further victimization by local leaders, mostly male. But they remain reluctant to call attention to their troubles for fear of exposing their communities to contempt or their families to intervention by outsiders.

Aboriginal people who asked the Commission to help end the violence had clear ideas about how it should be done:

- Don't stereotype all Aboriginal people as violent – make sure that interventions are targeted to those at risk.
- Don't let anyone use cultural difference as an excuse for violence – hold perpetrators accountable and make sure that the vulnerable are protected.
- Don't imagine that violence can be treated as a stand-alone problem – root out the social and political injustices, the poverty and the racism, that breed violence in all its forms.

These should be the first steps in making change:

- Aboriginal leaders should take a firm public stand against violence and work with their communities to develop zero tolerance standards and policies.

Well the problems I see in this town are water pollution, alcoholism and the school. Well for water pollution people are throwing wast in the water and its killing our animals. Now for alcoholism ever one is drinking and accidents are occuring well not all the time but its happening. Also the kids are running around town after midnight. Now for the school there is not enough class rooms the High school is using the science labs for the class room. Also there is no discipline in this school because there is over 50 school drop outs that should be in school, and also the school supplies always run out in the middle of the year. But I lived here all my life and I love it here.

Lily Cardinal

■ Aboriginal governments and organizations
should assure the full and fair representation
of women in decision making.
■ Aboriginal governments should support the
work Aboriginal women are doing to solve
health and social problems and recognize
their expertise in relation to family violence.

Some Aboriginal people are wary of giving
their own governments scope to interfere in family life, as Canadian governments have done in
the past. But there is an undeniable need to protect the vulnerable. It is a matter of balance.

THE URGENT NEED
FOR WHOLE HEALTH

The health status of Aboriginal people in Canada
today is both a tragedy and a crisis. Illness of
almost every kind occurs more often among
Aboriginal people than among other Canadians.

■ Registered Indians (for whom we have the
best data) can expect to die 7 to 8 years
younger than other Canadians. This difference in life expectancy has two major causes: a
higher rate of death among Aboriginal babies
(twice the national average), and a higher rate
of injury and accidental death among
Aboriginal children, youth and young adults.
■ Infectious diseases of all kinds, from gas-
trointestinal infections to tuberculosis,
though less common than they once were,
still occur at higher rates among Aboriginal
people than among other Canadians.
■ Chronic and degenerative diseases such as
cancer and heart disease are affecting more
Aboriginal people than they once did.
Diabetes, with its many complications, is a
particularly serious problem in some places.
■ Rates of violence and self-destructive behaviour, including substance abuse and suicide,
are high.
■ Elevated rates of educational failure, unemployment, welfare dependency, conflict with
the law and incarceration signal major imbal-
ances in the life experience and well-being of
Aboriginal people.

Twenty-five years of effort by local, provincial and national health caregivers have raised
Aboriginal health status from the lows to which it

had sunk by mid-century. Still, the results fall far short of the goal of equal health outcomes for all Canadians.

Aboriginal people urgently need resources to help them reduce infant mortality, tuberculosis, diabetes, heart disease and other illnesses. But they know that curing diseases of the body alone cannot restore well-being. What they are looking for is more fundamental and more transformative.

They are trying to bring balance and vitality to body, mind, emotions and spirit – as ends in themselves and as preconditions for balance and vitality in their societies. In short, they are looking for whole health.

Historical records and archaeological evidence tell us that many of the illnesses prevalent in Europe at the time of first contact were unknown or very rare in the Americas. Infectious diseases, from influenza to tuberculosis, were passed from the newcomers to Indigenous people, with devastating results. Hundreds of thousands sickened and died. In Canada, a population estimated at 500,000 at the time of first contact had plunged to 102,000 by the time of the 1871 census.

In the new climate of social responsibility that sparked the growth of public services after the Second World War, health authorities began to take seriously the need for medical care in Aboriginal communities. Today, almost every settlement has at least nursing services available. But despite large sums spent on illness care, Aboriginal people still experience ill health at unacceptable levels. The Commission looked at

- infant, child and maternal health
- infectious disease
- chronic disease
- disability
- injury and accident
- alcohol abuse
- community health (poverty, physical living conditions, environmental hazards)

In each case, although gains have been made, disadvantage continues. In each case, too, the pattern of causality for a specific illness includes factors outside the boundaries of ordinary medicine – social, emotional and economic conditions

More illness care services will not turn the tide.

Wellness is a community issue, a national issue, a women's issue... No other [issue] so fundamentally relates to the survival of our people as that of health.

Vice-Chief Tom Iron
Federation of Saskatchewan
Indian Nations
Wahpeton, Saskatchewan

Diabetes, hypertension, overweight, poor nutritional status are epidemic among Native people in Canada today.

Elizabeth Palfrey
Keewatin Regional
Health Board
Rankin Inlet,
Northwest Territories

A SIGNIFICANT CHALLENGE *is how to communicate the complex relationship between the structural conditions of Aboriginal people's lives – the economics and the politics – and their health and well-being. The heart of the matter was well summarized by Peter Penashue, an Innu leader from Labrador, in a speech to a Conference on Circumpolar Health more than 10 years ago:*

The Innu are sick and dying because of a well-documented syndrome of ill health brought on by the enforced dependency and attempted acculturation of an entire people. This ill health will improve or worsen, not according to the...level of health care funding, but only as a result of a political choice by those who now [control] Innu and Innu lives...

The fact is, that for the Innu, health and ill health are profoundly political issues, inseparable from social and economic considerations. The arrival of an elaborate health care system among the Innu coincided with a rapid worsening of Innu health. This is not to imply that one led to the other, but rather to emphasize that the health or ill health of the Innu has been [determined] by factors that have very little to do with the health care system...

The World Health Organization has recognized that individual good health can best be assured through maintenance of healthy socio-economic and cultural systems – and that, conversely, the exploitation and humiliation of societies will inevitably lead to both collective and individual ill health. For the Innu, the real health system will be the one which will allow Innu society to function properly again – one which will remove foreign domination, and one which will offer the Innu respect as a distinct people.

that in turn lead back to the complex, destabilizing and demoralizing legacy of colonialism.

Obviously, then, more of the same – more illness care services – will not turn the tide. What is needed is a new strategy for Aboriginal health and healing.

Two Traditions of Healing Converge

In recent years, Aboriginal people have shown great energy and imagination in tackling health and social problems. They have petitioned for more control of local services, and some have met with at least partial success. Those with partial control are beginning to modify and adapt services to reflect their own values, traditions and priorities – with good results.

But Aboriginal people want to make more radical changes in the way health and healing are promoted in their communities. Their main concerns revolve around four themes:

■ **Inequality of health status**
The rate of many illnesses, and the risk of future illness and premature death, are significantly higher among Aboriginal people than among

For a person to be healthy [he or she] must be adequately fed, be educated, have access to medical facilities, have access to spiritual comfort, live in a warm and comfortable house with clean water and safe sewage disposal, be secure in cultural identity, have an opportunity to excel in a meaningful endeavour, and so on. These are not separate needs; they are all aspects of a whole.

Henry Zoe
Dogrib Treaty 11 Council
Brief to the Commission

In the past, we were like we were asleep. White people were doing everything for us. We thought white people knew everything, but we were wrong. The advice they gave us never worked.

Chief Katie Rich
Davis Inlet
Sheshatshiu, Labrador

other Canadians. A further source of inequality favours some Aboriginal people over others: federal services and programs are available to registered Indians and Inuit, but not to others. But the fundamental inequality that puts Aboriginal people at risk for illness is income. Poverty and ill health go hand in hand, and Aboriginal people are among the poorest in Canada.

■ Interconnectedness

Aboriginal concepts of health and healing start from the position that all the elements of life and living are interdependent. By extension, well-being flows from balance and harmony among all elements of personal and collective life.

■ Control

Dependence on the Canadian state has left Aboriginal communities and nations without the authority to develop and control health and social services. Lack of control over important dimensions of living in itself contributes to ill health. Aboriginal people want to exercise their own judgement and understanding about what makes people healthy, their own skills in solving health and social problems.

■ Culture and traditional healing

Although Aboriginal people have moved far away from the lifestyles of their ancestors, they still see value in the traditions and practices that made them unique – including medical traditions ranging from herbal therapies to forms of psychotherapy. Often, they find that mainstream health services do not understand or fully meet their needs. They want to re-examine practices that were once suppressed or ridiculed for their possible usefulness today.

The most advanced thinkers in health policy circles today have reached some major conclusions about what makes people well. These 'determinants of health' converge with Aboriginal perspectives on health and healing through several key ideas:

- Health comes from the connectedness of human systems – body, mind, emotions, spirit – not their separate dynamics.
- Economic factors (employment status, personal and community poverty) play a central role in determining health.

- Personal responsibility for health and well-ness is as important as professional or external expertise.
- The health of the environment affects the health of people.
- Health and well-being in childhood affect lifelong health status.

These ideas favour a system that places less emphasis on particular medical conditions and more emphasis on the underlying social, economic and political factors that influence health.

Health policy must assist in dispelling the legacy of poverty, powerlessness and despair in Aboriginal communities. This is the key to whole health for Aboriginal people.

A Strategy for Health and Healing

Whole health comes from shared prosperity, a clean and safe environment, a sense of control over life circumstances – as well as high quality illness care and healthy lifestyle choices. Better

health for Aboriginal people will grow out of the long-term structural changes proposed in Chapter 2.

In the short term, however, prevention, treatment and rehabilitation services have an important contribution. Clearly, they can be improved. The starting place for reform is a commitment from federal, provincial, territorial and Aboriginal governments to build health and healing systems that do four things:

- pass the levers of control to Aboriginal people

What outside forces cannot bring about, Aboriginal people can do for themselves.

■ take a holistic approach to personal and social health

■ provide diverse services that respond to the cultures and priorities of Aboriginal people and to the special dynamics of Aboriginal ill health

■ bring equality in health status to Aboriginal people

Commitments must be turned into practical strategies if they are to change health outcomes. We propose a four-prong strategy, to be undertaken immediately:

1. Reorganization of existing health and social services into a system of health and healing centres and healing lodges, under Aboriginal control.

2. A crash program over the next 10 years to educate and train Aboriginal people to staff and manage health and social services at all levels, in Aboriginal communities and in mainstream institutions.

3. Adaptation of mainstream services to accommodate Aboriginal people as clients and as full participants in decision making.

4. A community infrastructure program to deal with urgent problems of housing, clean water and waste management.

Health and Healing Centres

The idea of community-based centres to develop and deliver integrated health and social services was put forward at our public hearings all over the country.

Health and healing centres can assemble, under one roof, the resources needed to tackle interrelated problems now dealt with typically by separate agencies – from child protection to mental health care. They can deliver medical care, make referrals to specialists, devise and deliver health promotion programs. In short, they can be the hub of health and social services in Aboriginal communities.

The kernel of such a system already exists – nursing stations and other facilities that co-ordinate at least some health and healing services in First Nations and Inuit communities. But not all communities have even the beginnings of a healing centre. In rural Métis settlements and in small towns with a substantial Aboriginal population, there is a virtual vacuum of services designed for, and run by, Aboriginal people. This vacuum needs to be filled.

To complement the work of community-based healing centres, the Commission proposes a network of healing lodges. Healing lodges can fill the acute need for residential treatment for people overwhelmed by social, emotional and spiritual distress. They can take up the issues of psycho-social distress that impair the lives of some Aboriginal people. For example, they could serve

■ victims of family violence who need a safe place and time to re-orient their lives
■ abusive adults who need to learn new ways of dealing with frustration and anger
■ alienated youth who need to reconnect with their communities and their identity

The seed of this second part of the system is existing Aboriginal-run drug and alcohol treatment facilities. Many have already gone a long way toward programming for whole health.

Getting a start on healing centres and healing lodges does not depend on the structural changes in governance and land we talked about in the previous chapter. It does depend on the will to abandon fruitless debates about which level of government is responsible for which services.

Human Resources Development

No amount of intervention from outsiders, however well meant, will help Aboriginal people achieve well-being. What outside forces cannot bring about, Aboriginal people can do for themselves. They can make the best decisions about the kind of health and healing services that will restore them to whole health – and they can do the work of making healing centres and lodges a success.

Very few Aboriginal people are now practising as doctors, nurses, social workers, nutritionists or psychologists. This is a problem in itself, but the problem goes deeper. Services aimed at whole health need to be culture-based and holistic – integrated across the full range of life problems.

The key to better integration of health and social services in Aboriginal communities is an increase in the number of professionals originating from those communities...
　　　　Huguette Blouin
　　　　Quebec hospitals
　　　　association
　　　　Montreal, Quebec

Centres and lodges need service providers with special skills and abilities.

■ One pressing need is people who can apply Aboriginal knowledge to current health problems and combine traditional health and healing practices with mainstream approaches to build distinctive Aboriginal healing systems.

■ Another is Aboriginal people trained to work in mainstream services – as professional care-givers, managers, board members and informed consumers – to help serve Aboriginal clients and to affirm the Aboriginal presence in Canadian life.

We propose that governments and educational institutions undertake to train 10,000 Aboriginal people for careers in the health and social services, including the full range of professional and managerial roles, over the next 10 years.

Enlisting Support from Mainstream Institutions

Aboriginal health and healing centres are only part of the picture. Most Aboriginal people will, at least occasionally, continue to consult practitioners and use facilities in mainstream agencies and institutions – from doctors and hospitals to sheltered workshops for people with disabilities and transition houses for victims of family violence.

The institutions that deliver human services need to become more sensitive to the distinctive health and healing needs of Aboriginal people. Even when Aboriginal people are a major part of the client base, hospitals and other institutions are slow to adapt their practices to Aboriginal needs. Cultural sensitivity and responsiveness that go beyond the superficial should become a priority.

Mainstream institutions also have a role in supporting the development of new Aboriginal institutions. Even in tough economic times, the resources of mainstream institutions are vast compared to those under Aboriginal control. It is reasonable to expect them to offer some help to fledgling Aboriginal services.

Aboriginal institutions will welcome assistance in developing efficient and effective systems – as long as they can get it without relinquishing their autonomy. They will be looking for

- training opportunities
- mentoring and support for new staff
- back-up and specialist services
- access to specialized equipment and similar resources

At the same time, mainstream institutions and professionals can learn from Aboriginal ways of promoting whole health.

We suggest that all organizations involved in delivering health and social services to Aboriginal people undertake a systematic assessment of their practices to see how they can improve their connections with Aboriginal people.

Infrastructure Development

The fourth strand of the strategy for attaining whole health is an infrastructure program – to bring housing, water supplies and waste manage-

We have families...doubled and tripled up. We have up to 18 and 20 people sometimes, living in a single unit built for one family.

Valerie Monague
Social services
administrator, Christian
Island, Ontario

[Because] low-income Native families have no other place to go...the slum landlords in town are doing a great business.

Martin Heavy Head
Chair, Treaty 7 Urban
Housing Authority
Lethbridge, Alberta

ment in Aboriginal communities up to generally accepted Canadian standards of health and safety. Immediate threats to health and well-being from flimsy and overcrowded houses, polluted water and untreated sewage are so serious that solutions cannot wait. More details on this problem and how to solve it are presented in the next section.

HOUSING AND LIVING CONDITIONS: MEETING URGENT NEEDS

Despite significant public spending over the past decade, housing, water supplies and sanitation services for Aboriginal people fall far below Canadian standards in many communities. Overcrowded and dilapidated houses, unclean and limited supplies of water, inadequate disposal of human wastes – these conditions pose an unacceptable threat to the health of Aboriginal people and reinforce feelings of marginalization and hopelessness.

■ Houses occupied by Aboriginal people are twice as likely to be in need of major repairs as those of other Canadians. On reserves, 13,400 homes need such repairs, and 6,000 need outright replacement.

■ Aboriginal homes are generally smaller than those of other Canadians, but more people live in them.
■ Aboriginal homes are 90 times more likely than those of other Canadians to be without piped water. On reserves, more than 10,000 homes have no indoor plumbing.
■ About one reserve community in four has a substandard water or sewage system.
■ In the North, solid waste dumps and untreated sewage are contaminating earth, land, fish and animals.

Ensuring that Aboriginal people have safe housing and adequate water and sewage services should be a high priority for government action – first, to reduce threats to health and second, to avoid saddling new nation governments with a shelter and services crisis. There are several long-standing impediments to action:

■ The cost of meeting the full needs of Aboriginal people for shelter, water and sanitation services is high, and governments are reluctant to accept it.

First Nations argue that the provision of housing and services is a treaty right. The federal government disagrees.

Construction in rural and northern communities, where many Aboriginal people live, is technically difficult and therefore costly. The housing market is too small and too dependent on the fortunes of resource industries to work well.

Financing for new construction through banks and other lending institutions is difficult to arrange on reserves because of restrictions in the *Indian Act* and confusion about individual home ownership.

The coming of self-government offers a golden opportunity to recast national, provincial and territorial policies governing Aboriginal housing and community services. As it stands, governments are simply not keeping up with desperate need. In some cases, they have cut useful assistance programs before they met their targets.

Until Aboriginal nations can take over the field, Canadian governments have an obligation to ensure adequate shelter for all Aboriginal people.

Most Aboriginal people can make a contribution – some by taking on mortgage responsibilities, others by supplying labour or materials for construction and repairs or paying rent for existing units. This they should do, to the fullest extent possible, to free up scarce funds to help those in greatest need.

We propose that Canadian and Aboriginal governments, and Aboriginal people as individuals, contribute resources enough to ensure that housing needs are fully met within 10 years. The long-standing bones of contention standing in the way of action can be solved as follows:

We believe that Aboriginal people and communities should help to meet their housing costs. We propose that federal and provincial/territorial governments take on about two-thirds of housing costs and Aboriginal people, once they reach a certain income level, take on about one-third.

Regional Aboriginal institutions can be established to manage the financing, con-

We are forced to dump our sewage in open pits and use outdoor privies at 30 to 40 below, winter temperatures. This practice causes people of all ages to get sick.

Chief Ignace Gull
Attawapiskat First Nation community
Moose Factory, Ontario

struction and maintenance of homes and community infrastructure.

■ The issue of the treaty right to housing can be dealt with in the new treaty processes we propose.

■ The issue of home ownership on reserves should fall under the jurisdiction of new Aboriginal nation governments and should be resolved in a way that provides incentives for residents to maintain and improve their homes.

As for water and sanitation, the federal government's Green Plan (a special initiative that ended in 1995) went some way toward closing the gap in basic services between Aboriginal and non-Aboriginal communities. But the job is not yet done.

Current federal projections lay out a timetable of at least nine years before all substandard facilities can be repaired or replaced. This is simply not fast enough for so fundamental a determinant of health and community morale.

Most of the communities with acute water and sanitation needs are small. Bringing their services up to standard will not require complicated technology or a big bureaucracy. It will require appropriate technology, adequate funding and knowledgeable, well-trained people to operate and monitor essential services.

We propose doubling the speed of remediation, so that all communities will have adequate water and sanitation services within 5 years.

Just as poor housing and services have harmful effects on health and well-being, so a turnaround in this sector could have broadly regenerative effects. For example,

- Building and maintaining homes, water lines, pumping stations, sewage treatment plants and so on will create new demand for local labour, skills and enterprise. The 10-year home-building and repair effort we recommend is expected to generate 178,000 person years of employment in the construction sector alone. It will also give local contractors experience they can apply to expanding their businesses.

- Communities will be able to pool their building requirements, creating still more possibilities. For example, the needs of a group of communities could support a cement company and other specialized businesses.

- Other economic spin-off effects could be greater still. Federal, provincial and territorial governments should be ready with equity capital to help stimulate local businesses in concert with the housing boom.

Home building is more than assembling bricks and boards. In Oujé-Bougoumou, Quebec, a project to build new houses, using traditional culture and values along with modern design and technology, became the starting point for community healing and renewal. Just a decade ago, the living conditions of the Cree of Oujé-Bougoumou were described as "the worst in the developed world". Today, their situation has improved to the point where the United Nations recently chose their new village as one of 50 exemplary communities around the world.

It can be done.

THE GESGAPEGIAG FIRST NATION community in eastern Quebec has developed an active housing program using government subsidies and credit from the local Caisse Populaire Desjardins. The band negotiates loans for residents willing and able to take on a mortgage and also trains and provides local labour to keep construction costs down.

Aboriginal Control of Aboriginal Education: Still Waiting

Aboriginal people often say, "Our children are our future." By extension, then, the future depends on the effectiveness of education. Education shapes the pathways of thinking, transmits values as well as facts, teaches language and social skills, helps release creative potential, and determines productive capacities.

Aboriginal people are well aware of the power of education. Greater control over their children's education has been a demand for at least three decades.

Parental involvement and local control of schools are standard practice in Canada – but not for Aboriginal people. Instead, they have long been the object of attempts by state and church authorities to use education to control and assimilate them, during the residential school era, certainly, but also, more subtly, today.

By seeking greater control over schooling, Aboriginal people are asking for no more than

what other communities already have: the chance to say what kind of people their children will become. In the main, Aboriginal people want two things from education:

- They want schools to help children, youth and adults learn the skills they need to participate fully in the economy.
- They want schools to help children develop as citizens of Aboriginal nations – with the knowledge of their languages and traditions necessary for cultural continuity.

The present education system does not accomplish either of these goals. The majority of Aboriginal youth do not finish high school. They leave with neither the credentials for jobs in the mainstream economy nor a grounding in their languages and cultures. They are very likely to have experienced the ignorance and hatred of racism, which leaves them profoundly demoralized or angered.

Many of our proposals for change in education have been advanced before, by commissions and task forces stretching back to the 1970s. It is clear what needs to be done, and it is long past time to do it.

- Transfer of administrative responsibility for reserve schools to First Nations is a step in

As we work towards establishing Anishnabe political systems, we need to give attention to education as a way of achieving functioning Anishnabe nations...

Vernon Roote
Deputy Grand Chief,
Union of Ontario Indians

the right direction. But schools are still staffed primarily by non-Aboriginal teachers, and curriculums and teaching methods were designed for students with different needs and cultural backgrounds.

- Almost 70 per cent of Aboriginal children are taught in provincial or territorial schools, but the mainstream education system has few mechanisms of accountability to Aboriginal people and has made few attempts to reach out and involve Aboriginal parents.
- In all jurisdictions, spending on Aboriginal education is inadequate to reverse accumulated educational deficits.

Even so, Aboriginal people retain their conviction that education can be a positive force in the pursuit of bicultural competence and confidence for their children and themselves. They believe that education can contribute to the holistic development of Aboriginal people of all ages, from infants to elders.

To this end, we recommend the development of Aboriginal-controlled education systems, recognized by all governments and able to plan and deliver lifelong learning. Further, we are recommending that provincial and territorial schools take steps to ensure that the education they provide is fully appropriate for their Aboriginal students.

Education policy needs to ensure that appropriate learning takes place at each stage in the life cycle.

Early Childhood Education

In education, as in health, childhood is the foundational stage. Traditional family life provided a firm foundation of security and encouragement for Aboriginal children. Aboriginal families of today are not always able to provide this. Parents may be hampered by the effects of poverty, alienation, residential school experience, and dysfunctional family or other relationships. Many Aboriginal children arrive at school with special needs for understanding and support to liberate their in-born capacity for learning.

Like all children, Aboriginal children need to

Aboriginal education as assimilation has always, everywhere, failed and failed miserably and failed destructively... Aboriginal education for self-determination, controlled by Aboriginal people, succeeds.

Dr. Eber Hampton
President, Saskatchewan
Indian Federated College

master the intellectual, physical, emotional and spiritual tasks of early childhood. Equally, they need grounding in their identity as Aboriginal people. We propose that all Aboriginal children, regardless of status or location, have access to dynamic, culture-based early childhood education. For elementary schools, we propose that

- all schools, whether or not they serve mainly Aboriginal students, adopt curriculums that reflect Aboriginal cultures and realities
- governments allocate resources such that Aboriginal language instruction can be given high priority, where numbers warrant
- provincial and territorial schools make greater efforts to involve Aboriginal parents in decision making

Education for Youth

Aboriginal adolescents straddle two worlds – one where Aboriginal values and beliefs prevail, and another where television, popular culture and peer pressure offer competing values and priorities.

Aboriginal teenagers need a secure sense of self-worth to keep their balance in the storm of conflicting messages and demands. Many have

not found that balance. Their confusion and distress are evident in high drop-out rates, teen pregnancy, substance abuse, defiance of the law and suicidal behaviour.

Aboriginal youth who spoke to the Commission said that they felt marginalized – unable to make their voices heard at school or in their home communities. We discuss several ways of empowering them in the next chapter.

It is critically important for Aboriginal adolescents to be able to live at home while attending secondary school. At age 13, they are not prepared for life away from a family and cultural base. Eventually, high school should be available in all Aboriginal communities. Where communities are very small, distance education may help make local high school programs possible.

Aboriginal youth who drop out before graduating need support and encouragement to return to school later. This is especially important for young women who leave because of pregnancy. Aboriginal and provincial authorities should take steps to make school re-entry easier and more attractive to Aboriginal youth.

Education for Adults

Many Aboriginal people reach adulthood without the skills, knowledge or credentials they need to find jobs or take up positions of responsibility in their communities. Their needs range from basic literacy and numeracy to advanced professional training. Federal, provincial and territorial governments have sponsored a range of adult training programs, but Aboriginal candidates face special barriers:

- Too few programs are accessible in or near their often remote communities.
- Courses lack relevance to their lives and circumstances.
- Entry requirements are insensitive to their backgrounds and cultures.
- Programs offer few of the personal supports they need, especially child care for adult women students.

Aboriginal colleges, such as the Saskatchewan Indian Federated College, Old Sun in Alberta and the Nicola Valley Institute of Technology in British Columbia, have grown up to meet some of these needs. Most are small, community-based institutions that tailor their programs to adult learners whose previous experience of schooling

may have been very bad. They have proved themselves able to retain students until they graduate, often with high levels of achievement.

All governments should co-operate to increase the number of these institutions, to put them on a stable financial footing, and to secure their place in the post-secondary system.

Mainstream colleges and universities see high drop-out rates among their Aboriginal students. To improve retention, barriers to success must be dismantled. Students may require assistance to qualify for entry to colleges and universities, and they may require special supports to stay the course. Models of support can be found in a number of provinces and institutions.

Aboriginal nations will want to pursue funding for post-secondary education in their treaty negotiations. In the meantime, the federal government should continue to pay the full cost of post-secondary education for status Indians. It should also provide a special post-secondary scholarship and assistance fund for Métis and non-status Indian students.

The Splats'in Daycare Centre of the Spallumcheen First Nation in British Columbia was designed on a traditional, extended family model. Elders and children participated in everyday activities such as caring for animals, cultivating a garden and doing traditional crafts together. Through daily exposure to the Shuswap language, the children started to become Aboriginal language speakers.

Education for Self-Government

Aboriginal people and nations need the right kind of education to make self-government a reality and a success. First, they need an array of trained people for the jobs that will be created. Second, they need educational institutions to safeguard and advance their cultures, languages and knowledge bases and to apply traditional knowledge to the problems of the modern world. These needs can best be met by institutions operating at the regional or national level.

The most pressing need is for trained people. The availability of these resources varies from one Aboriginal nation to another. But all nations face growing demands for skilled managers and staff to fill a range of public service jobs: jobs in economic development, health and social services, public works, education, sports and recreation, and so on.

Detailed forecasts of personnel needs will emerge from planning by Aboriginal nations, but it is safe to say that there are not enough trained Aboriginal people to fill the posts that will be available.

The Commission proposes that Aboriginal nations investigate and establish targets for human resources development in key fields and that Canadian governments enter into partnership with them to offer flexible training opportunities, internships and exchange programs to achieve targets in designated areas. Governments should co-operate to mount a campaign to make Aboriginal youth aware of the opportunities soon to be available. The time for these steps is not after treaties and other agreements are in place but before, so Aboriginal nations are as ready as they can be to implement self-government. Education is a key ingredient in readiness.

As Aboriginal nation governments are put in place, they will increasingly take charge of planning and delivering lifelong learning to their citizens, co-ordinating their efforts with provincial and territorial institutions. Aboriginal education authorities are already being run by some local communities. The Nisg̱a'a in British Columbia and the Mi'kmaq in N̄ova Scotia have signed agreements establishing comprehensive education authorities for their nations. Our recommendations encourage this trend.

We also recommend education measures to protect and develop Aboriginal cultures:

■ The Aboriginal Peoples International University

An Aboriginal-controlled university is the institution of choice to protect and extend traditional knowledge and to pursue applied research on issues of concern to Aboriginal nations. It would build on regional initiatives and promote collaboration among existing colleges. It would offer a co-ordinated network of courses and programs in First Nations, Métis and Inuit communities and through distance education.

■ An electronic clearinghouse

Despite the distances that separate them, Aboriginal people need to be able to communicate their experience of success and failure – in education reform and in all areas of self-management. It could take the form of a Canadian version of NativeNet in the United States, using the Internet.

The objectives of Métis self-government and economic development cannot be achieved in the absence of educated and technically trained individuals within our Métis communities...
Claire Riddle
Vice-President,
Winnipeg Region
Manitoba Metis Federation

A substantial portion of the history of Aboriginal people resides in government files, church store-rooms, and archives across Canada – the rest is safeguarded in the memories of Aboriginal people, many of whom are elders now. Records and recollections of history, both the good and the bad, should be collected, preserved and made more accessible to all Canadians, before it is too late. We see an Aboriginal-controlled documentation centre as the best way to do so.

PROTECTING ABORIGINAL ARTS AND HERITAGE

Traditional Aboriginal cultures embody complete ways of being in the world. Cultures are shaped by particular landscapes and guided by a philosophy that assigns life and spirit to everything in the circle of being. The Aboriginal conviction that all things have a place and a purpose and are connected in a web of interdependence is reflected in ethical codes meant to guide human behaviour toward balance.

Aboriginal cultures have never been static. They have always responded to the flow of human experience. They are not frozen in irrelevance; neither are they 'lost' or 'dead'.

More and more Aboriginal people are opening their hearts and minds to the relevance of traditional beliefs and practices for life in the modern world and to their powerful role in restoring a sense of self, collective identity, and purpose to those who have lost their way.

Because of past policies that ignored and suppressed Aboriginal languages, ceremonies and living traditions, Aboriginal cultures are endangered. Positive action is needed to help those seeking ways to express, conserve, restore and document their cultures, in all their richness and diversity.

Protective action should extend to the material forms of Aboriginal cultures (artifacts, works of art and craft, historical sites) and to their dynamic forms – songs, dances, stories and teachings that bring collective memory, insight and inspiration to Aboriginal people and to the world.

The living, changing cultures of Aboriginal peoples have an important role in helping to overturn the myths and stereotypes, twisted facts and misunderstandings that prevail in much of non-Aboriginal Canada. Doing so will require dialogue with knowledgeable Aboriginal communicators.

Knowledge of one another, and a sharing of wisdom, are essential to a true partnership of peoples.

Cultural Heritage

The cultures of Aboriginal peoples are tied to the land – to specific places held by tradition to have been given to them to care for and to supply what they need. Their histories and mythologies are tied to features of the landscape. The bones of their ancestors are buried there. With resources from the land, they have fashioned sacred objects for ceremonial purposes. They have carved masks and crests to record family histories and lineages

Still we survive, and we will continue to survive. Our language is still alive, as well as our culture, and we are very proud to be Indian.
Roly Williams
Noee Kwe Adult
Education Centre
London, Ontario

All along the Foothills, ceremonial leaders are spiritually guided to conduct ceremonies at specific sites, some of which are off-reserve, located on provincial or federal Crown lands. Our Elders are being denied full access...
Alvin Manitopyes
Assembly of First Nations
Environmental Committee

and told of memorable events in songs, stories and dances.

But Aboriginal people have lost control of many of their sacred sites. They have watched as objects of great power and significance were taken away by outsiders and displayed in distant museums, often out of context and in ways that offend their sacred value. Aboriginal people have made justifiable demands for

- protection of historical and sacred sites
- recovery of human remains for proper burial
- repatriation of artifacts of particular importance
- prevention of the appropriation (theft) of songs, stories and other intellectual property by non-Aboriginal people

Some site protection issues are being resolved as part of treaty making and renewal. Some museums and galleries have been willing to give back sacred objects. Some artists, writers and archaeologists are showing sensitivity to the use of Aboriginal images and stories. But the understanding shown by a few is not enough to protect cultural heritage as Aboriginal people desire.

Governments should co-operate in making an inventory of sacred sites, in part so that those threatened by development or natural erosion can be saved. Elders should be involved in identifying sites requiring urgent attention.

We also urge museums and cultural institutions to adopt ethical guidelines for the collection, display and interpretation of artifacts related to Aboriginal cultures. Aboriginal people need greater access to their own cultural heritage, more opportunities for cultural education, and increased resources to develop their own facilities for display and study.

Living Languages

Language is one of the main instruments for transmitting culture from one generation to another and for communicating meaning and making sense of collective experience.

In Canada, there are 11 Aboriginal language families and more than 50 different languages. The number of Aboriginal language speakers is only a fraction of the Aboriginal population: about one person in three over the age of five. Most are middle-aged or older. Even the languages in most frequent use – Mi'kmaq, Montagnais, Cree, Ojibwa, Inuktitut and some Dene languages – are in danger of extinction because of declining fluency in the young.

Minority languages all over the world are declining in the face of culturally dominant languages – especially those used in the media and popular culture. Aboriginal languages suffered a severe blow during the era when every child was forced by school policy to speak English or French.

The threat of their languages disappearing means that Aboriginal people's distinctive world view, the wisdom of their ancestors and their ways of being human could vanish as well.

Language is one of the main instruments for transmitting culture from one generation to another.

One Elder has said, 'Without the language, we are warm bodies without a spirit'.
Elder Mary Lou Fox
Ojibwe Cultural
Foundation
Sudbury, Ontario

I Lost My Talk
by Rita Joe

I lost my talk
The talk you took away.
When I was a little girl
At Shubenacadie school.

You snatched it away:
I speak like you
I think like you
I create like you
The scrambled ballad about my
world.

Two ways I talk
Both ways I say
Your way is more powerful.

So gently I offer my hand and ask,
Let me find my talk
So I can teach you about me.

Language protection requires

■ maintaining or increasing the number of flu-
ent speakers
■ using the language as a medium of communication in everyday life – especially in the
family

Where languages are declining or severely
threatened, school immersion programs can help
– but a language will not live if it is not used in
everyday life. It must be the medium of communication at work, in school, in the media, in government – and most of all, at home.

Each Aboriginal nation will have to decide
how far it can go in preserving its languages and
develop policies to match. In the meantime, the
speakers of Aboriginal languages are aging and
dying. We propose the establishment of an
Aboriginal Languages Foundation to document,
study and conserve Aboriginal languages and to
help Aboriginal people arrest and reverse the loss
of languages that has already occurred.

Communications

Canada has always been held together in part by
its communication links – from the river systems
of the fur traders to the transcontinental railroad
to the satellite signals linking us today. The information passing along these channels shapes and
defines our view of the world and of one another.
The need for accurate information and realistic
portrayals of Aboriginal people is evident.

But Aboriginal people are not well represented by or in the media. Many Canadians
know Aboriginal people only as noble environ-
mentalists, angry warriors or pitiful victims. A
full picture of their humanity is simply not available in the media.

Mainstream media do not reflect Aboriginal
realities very well. Nor do they offer much space
to Aboriginal people to tell their own stories – as
broadcasters, journalists, commentators, poets or
story tellers. Aboriginal people have little opportunity to tell Canadians in their own ways and
their own words who they are.

Because Canadians do not hear Aboriginal
points of view, they are often left with mistaken

impressions about Aboriginal people's lives and aspirations and the reasons for their actions.

Aboriginal people are also severely limited in their opportunities to communicate with one another. They have few media services of their own – and even those lost almost all their funding in recent cuts. Domination of the media by the imagery and preoccupations of non-Aboriginal people contributes to the weakening of Aboriginal cultures. In the North, for example, the arrival of television in the 1960s helped transform the society in just one generation.

We make proposals in four areas:

■ The Canadian Radio-Television and Telecommunications Commission should require those who hold broadcast licences in areas with significant Aboriginal populations to provide air time for an Aboriginal presence.

■ Mainstream media, both public and private, should provide for a greater Aboriginal presence in their offerings.

■ The federal government should support training of Aboriginal people for media positions.

■ The federal government should provide core funding for Aboriginal-controlled media and incentives for private support for these media.

Visual and Performing Arts

For Aboriginal people, as for all people, the arts are both a reflection and an extension of their history, mythology and spirituality. They are a mirror Aboriginal people hold up to see themselves more clearly and a window they hold open to let others see in. Whether they explore traditional forms of expression, modern forms or both, Aboriginal artists, performers and writers are contributing to their own cultures and to Canada's cultural identity as well.

Given their importance, it is perhaps surprising how little public or private support Aboriginal arts and artists actually receive.

■ The great majority of the books about Aboriginal people marketed each year by major Canadian publishers are written by non-Aboriginal authors.

■ Aboriginal publishers report difficulty securing support from government agencies that support publishing.

■ Aboriginal arts that were once part of everyday life and ceremonial use are relegated to the status of crafts and artifacts and housed predominantly in museums, rather than displayed in art galleries.

■ The Indian affairs department has been instrumental in creating a market for Inuit arts and crafts and provided general support for training in the visual and performing arts. But it offers minimal help in mounting productions, which are a crucial part of training.

■ Arts funding agencies are only beginning to look for ways to judge Aboriginal forms and artistic creations, at least in part according to culture-specific criteria.

The expression of Aboriginal voice, rooted in unique cultures and world views, was actively suppressed in the era of domination and assimilation. Even in this era of renewal, Aboriginal arts and artists are neglected by Canadian institutions, both public and private.

The Commission sees a need for active support for at least a generation, to encourage revitalization and development of visual, literary and performing arts. We propose establishment of an Aboriginal Arts Council, a review of granting criteria in mainstream institutions, and increased support for training and facilities for display and performance.

Among the Gitksan and Wet'suwet'en, there is no mother tongue word for health. However, they do have a word for strength, which is interchangeable [with] health. They also speak of well-being. This well-being is associated with high self-esteem, a feeling of being at peace and being happy... This includes education. It includes employment. It includes land claims. It includes resource management. All of these lead back to wellness and well-being.

Rhea Joseph
Native Brotherhood of B.C.
on Health Issues

Better Lives for Aboriginal People

Discussions of Aboriginal affairs sometimes seem weighted toward issues of governance, law, constitution making and institution building. But the real point of these mechanisms is to make Aboriginal lives better.

Over the years, much time and energy and many dollars have been spent trying to do this. Yet serious problems of ill health, miseducation and disturbed family life remain. Aboriginal people and communities are worn down by the persistence of these problems. Canadians feel them as a drag on national progress.

Are the social problems of Aboriginal people intransigent? Hopeless? Certainly not. But ways of organizing and delivering human services for Aboriginal people must change fundamentally.

Patterns of distress, violence and self-destructive behaviour will never shift fully toward well-being without a concomitant shift of power, control and resources. But Aboriginal control is not a panacea – self-government is not a magic wand, and it is no guarantee of good results. It is always possible that Aboriginal control will be

exercised badly from time to time. In any case, it will take time for self-government to have an impact.

In the meantime, improving the lives and strengthening the capacities of Aboriginal people is a worthwhile end in itself. It is also part of making Aboriginal control work, as illustrated by the circle of well-being described at the beginning of this chapter.

How can it be done? In four ways:

■ Canadian governments can make room for Aboriginal initiative and control.
■ Leaders at all levels can give greater prominence to social policy.
■ Human services can be shifted from piecemeal to holistic programming.
■ Individuals in need of housing, healing, schooling and other kinds of help can be provided for along the lines proposed by the Commission.

Everything in nature is sacred © 1992

"Two and a half million bison were destroyed each year between 1870-1875"

There were 60 million buffalo living on the abundant wild grasses of North America. Nowhere in the world, not even in Africa has there been a single large sacred animal in such abundance. The buffalo supplied the Indigenous native for centuries. At the Sun dance; altars are built to honour this great animal, The Buffalo.

Perspectives and Realities

4

The Aboriginal peoples of Canada include First Nations, Inuit and Métis peoples. The more than 50 First Nations have much in common, but they are different from one another – and very different from Inuit, whose culture was shaped by the demanding northern environment. Different again are Métis people, who blended traditions from Aboriginal and European forebears in a unique new culture.

MANY PEOPLES, MANY VOICES

In the first three chapters, we discussed many of the things that matter most to Aboriginal people. But it is misleading to imply that all Aboriginal people share identical concerns and priorities.

Some groups have concerns that cut across cultural and nation lines. Women, youth, elders, people living in cities and those living in the North have specific concerns and proposals for change, many of which they presented to the Commission. We recognize the multiple realities of Aboriginal peoples, and in this chapter we give them voice.

By grouping people and ideas in this way, we don't want to imply that all women or all Métis persons or all northerners agree on issues and solutions. They do not. But in our conversations with them, some dominant themes did emerge, and we present them here. We hope that everyone who spoke to us will find something of themselves in what follows.

VOICES OF WOMEN

Women played a prominent part in the political
and cultural life of many traditional Aboriginal
societies. First and foremost, they were honoured
as the givers of life. Their ability to bear, raise and
nurture the new generation was seen as a special
gift from the Creator, a source of awesome power
and equal responsibility.

Women's leadership roles varied from nation
to nation. Mohawk women, for example, were
active in the political life of clan, village, nation
and confederacy. Inuit women deferred to male
leaders in public decision making but had considerable influence in social relations and family
affairs, especially as they grew older. In some
Aboriginal societies, women had a more subordi-
nate role; even then, their skills and knowledge
gave them an essential role in the community.

We are under no illusion that women's lives
before contact were free of social problems. But
Aboriginal women told us that, with the coming
of colonial powers, a disturbing mind-set crept
into their own societies. Policies and laws
imposed by foreign governments ruptured cultural traditions and introduced discrimination
against women.

Today, Aboriginal women are organized in
ways that allow them to press for action on issues
that concern them. Largely silenced for many
years, now they will be heard.

Women and Indian Status

Their first concerns are for their immediate families and communities. But they have seen first-
hand how laws and policies can have devastating
consequences when put into action.

We have already described how Aboriginal
people were restricted and controlled by the
Indian Act and other laws originating in the nineteenth century. Women were doubly disadvantaged by the sexist nature of this law, rooted as it
was in Victorian ideas of race and patriarchy. For
much of this century, women were not allowed to
vote in band elections, could not own or inherit
property, and were treated as the 'property' of
their husbands in many contexts.

Perhaps most offensive of all, a woman's
identity as a First Nations person came to depend

on the status of her husband. Even if she spoke her Aboriginal language, practised the traditions of her nation, and raised her children in the ways of her people, she ceased to be 'Indian' – in the eyes of the government – the moment she married a non-Indian. By extension, her children also ceased to be 'Indian'.

Women and children who lost Indian status lost all the rights that went with it. Men who married non-Indians did not suffer the same penalties. After a decade of challenges by Aboriginal women, the government made an effort to correct the injustice by introducing Bill C-31 in 1985.

Bill C-31 allows for the reinstatement of those who lost Indian status under the old rules and gives Indian status to their children. However, the process and criteria for first-time registration are confusing – and still offensive, because authority to determine who can be recognized as a status Indian still lies with the federal government, not with Aboriginal people.

As well, the children of women reinstated under Bill C-31 are still treated less favourably

than those of men who married non-Indians before 1985. And children born of such unions after 1985 generally cannot pass their status on to their children.

Given enough time and enough marriages

outside status boundaries, 'status Indians' could disappear completely as a category.

A further problem is that Bill C-31 delegated authority to bands to determine who can become a band member and consequently who can live on reserve lands. Those who acquired or regained status under Bill C-31 are not automatically given band membership or the rights that go with it. Access to subsidized housing on reserves is hotly contested in some places. Bill C-31 women and their children may suffer materially as well as psychologically from exclusion enforced by band decisions.

Instead of solving the status question once and for all, Bill C-31 created new divisions and new fears. As we see it, the solutions should be found by Aboriginal people themselves, as part of the nation-building process outlined in Chapter 2. Definitions of membership – or citizenship – in Aboriginal nations are not the business of Canadian governments. However, Aboriginal women and their organizations must be assured

the resources to participate fully in this process, and in all aspects of nation building, before the federal government vacates the terrain.

A Priority on Healing

The need for Aboriginal people to heal from the consequences of domination, displacement and assimilation is perhaps the overarching concern of Aboriginal women. They have seen the social fabric of their communities severely damaged by mistaken policies. Many told us that healing must take place before self-government can succeed. As they put it, only healthy people and healthy communities can create healthy nations.

Breaking free of the pain, anger and resentment that are the legacy of the colonial past means allowing Aboriginal people and communities to initiate their healing strategies – initiatives that draw on traditional practices and an understanding of people's needs. They want more and better community health and social services, with adequate resources and a preponderance of Aboriginal staff.

Family violence is a particularly alarming manifestation of the erosion of traditional norms of interpersonal respect. Many women spoke to us of fear for the safety of their children and themselves and the need for places of refuge. In some communities, especially smaller ones, it can be hard for a woman and her children to find a safe haven.

Aboriginal women want to see their leaders and communities take a zero-tolerance stand against family violence. They see a great need for more culturally appropriate counselling services for both perpetrators and victims.

Voices of Elders

Elders are known by many names in Aboriginal societies: the Old Ones, the Wise Ones, Grandmothers and Grandfathers and, in the Métis Nation, Senators. They are teachers, philosophers, linguists, historians, healers, judges, counsellors – all these roles and more.

Elders are living embodiments of Aboriginal traditions and cultures. Through the Creator's gifts and their years of walking the earth, they have acquired knowledge and experience to live well and thrive in the physical world. They are in tune with the land, the cycles and rhythms of nature and life.

Elders are keepers of spiritual knowledge that has sustained people through thousands of years – knowledge of ceremonies and traditional activities, of laws and rules set down by the Creator to enable the people to live as a nation.

Both types of knowledge are equally important and valid. The spiritual and the physical intertwine; the natural and the supernatural wrap like a braid around the daily act of living. The realm of the sacred becomes a part of everyday life.

Not all elders are seniors, nor are all old people elders. Some are quite young. But elders have gifts of insight and understanding, as well as communication skills to pass on the collective wisdom of generations that have gone before.

Elders do not hoard their knowledge. Their most important task is to pass it on, so that the culture of their people can stay vital and respon-

They live the culture, they know the culture, and they have been trained in it. These are the true elders.
Elder Vern Harper
Toronto, Ontario

The human voice leaves a lasting imprint on human memory and feelings, because so much heart and spirit can be communicated through the voice, like no other medium.
Esther Jacko
in *Voices: Being Native in Canada* (1992)

sive to changing times and conditions. The continuity of their nations depends on them.

They transmit culture and mores through action, example and oral tradition – stories, jokes, games and other shared activities. The experience is personal; speaker and listener share the event. Hearing stories and teachings, listeners feel the pain, the joy, the victories and defeats of their people. They reach out to one another across time. Past, present and future become one.

With the help of their elders, Aboriginal nations have struggled to maintain their traditional values, languages and knowledge base – despite aggressive external forces vying to destroy them. Aboriginal people have fought fiercely to preserve their traditions, knowing that they are the principal source of their identity, self-respect and strength as individuals and as nations.

Today we see a great resurgence of interest among Aboriginal people in their languages and traditions, many of which were fading until recently. Presenters at our public hearings told us that new institutions must build on the core teachings of Aboriginal tradition and the contemporary insights of the elders.

But reviving and reintroducing tradition does not mean turning back the clock. Most of the world's people live their lives according to religions and philosophies that are hundreds or thousands of years old. Similarly, Aboriginal traditions and teachings took their first form long ago, but they can be reshaped to be useful in the modern world.

The success of elders working with Aboriginal prisoners illustrates one part they can play. When we spoke to Aboriginal offenders, they told us how elders have helped them understand themselves, how they used counselling and traditional ceremonies to help them with the inner problems that contribute to criminal behaviour. Elders have been valuable in other judicial initiatives as well, especially in sentencing circles.

Elders told us that they have much more to offer than they are now being asked to give. They can be (and in some cases already are) significant contributors in education, health and social services, land and resource management boards, and

Elders are living embodiments of Aboriginal traditions and cultures.

Our vision is to be happy. We want to relax and have dreams and laugh. We want to love and talk... We want to know our Native culture. We want to respect each other. We have to have a better future.
Robert Quill
Merritt, British Columbia

We don't need money all the time. What we need is our nations, our people, our communities to come together as one and to work together as one, to sit down and say, 'Okay, this is what we've got to do.'
Stan Wesley
Moose Factory, Ontario

efforts to build Aboriginal governments. They can contribute at almost every stage and every level. In education, for example, much is lost if elders are merely brought into classrooms once a year for a 'cultural awareness' day. They could be helping to reshape curriculum, teaching practices and administration styles.

Aboriginal people want to see the ways of their ancestors recognized, protected and used. Elders must have access to sacred sites for ceremonies and to gather traditional plants and herbs. Elders, in turn, will contribute their gifts of insight and knowledge to the nation. This is as it should be, for elders are essential to the perpetuation and renewal of the Aboriginal way of life.

VOICES OF YOUTH

Aboriginal youth make up the largest segment of the Aboriginal population. An estimated 56.2 per cent of Aboriginal people are under 25. These young people will carry on the initiatives and live the dreams of Aboriginal nations in the next millennium.

Some of the most dynamic presentations we heard were from youth. They showed insight and heartening optimism in discussing the many serious issues affecting their life chances. They are looking for solutions that are practical and can be implemented right now in their communities. They are undaunted by political and administrative hurdles. They want to get the job done in the quickest, most effective way possible.

But youth do not feel their visions and ideas are being recognized by their leaders. They see themselves as a wasted resource. They urged Aboriginal organizations to follow the lead of the National Association of Friendship Centres and the Inuit Circumpolar Conference, to take steps to involve them more deeply in all community matters.

Aboriginal youth described three overarching goals for the future:

■ **Recognition and involvement.** They want to participate more fully in community and nation life and to work together with their peers in other Aboriginal nations on issues of common concern.

■ **Empowerment**. Youth want the tools and skills to solve their own problems. They talked to us about their wish for political empowerment, which means having a voice at the local, provincial and national levels of governance. They talked about economic empowerment as well, for they know they need jobs to break the cycle of dependence in which some of their kin have been trapped.

■ **Healing**. In harmony with Aboriginal women, youth saw healing as a necessary first step to their personal empowerment. They spoke about healing the spirit, the mind, the emotions and the body.

Spiritual healing and rediscovery are necessary so that Aboriginal youth can get a firm footing in their cultures and traditions. This will protect them from the alienation and hopelessness that lead to drug taking, lawlessness and suicidal behaviour. The Commission supports the call by young people for more opportunities to

learn about their cultures – not just as abstractions or relics but as living, growing traditions.

Healing of the mind implies a school environment in which the contributions of Aboriginal peoples to Canada and the world are studied, respected and validated. Youth need a curriculum inclusive of Aboriginal history and present-day realities. They need learning institutions run by Aboriginal people for Aboriginal people. They need better financial support to undertake and complete their studies.

Healing of the emotions can perhaps best be done with the help of elders. Aboriginal youth see elders as being able to offer them counselling in times of trouble from a contemporary perspective, informed by a traditional worldview. At the same time, they need to create space for serious talk among themselves and to share the emotional load that comes with being Aboriginal in Canada today.

Healing of the body completes the circle. Young people need more opportunities for sport and recreation, to help them build social bonds in their communities, create bridges to other communities, and develop leadership and team-playing capacities. Some told us that the social problems they see around them could be alleviated through recreation programs designed with these goals in mind.

Aboriginal youth are now served – not very well – in a piecemeal way by programs and initiatives of various departments and governments. We see a need for a co-ordinated, Canada-wide policy framework to deal with the concerns of Aboriginal youth – to take an integrated approach to issues of education, justice, health and healing, employment, sport and recreation, and urban concerns.

Although those who spoke to the Commission were largely optimistic about what lies ahead for them, Aboriginal youth face many obstacles to a safe and satisfying future. With a little help, they are ready to roll up their sleeves and do their part to refashion the future.

VOICES OF MÉTIS PEOPLE

Some 139,000 Canadians identify themselves as Métis. Their history dates back hundreds of years, but most Canadians know little about them. Métis are distinct Aboriginal peoples, with their own history, language and culture.

European fur traders and settlers began to associate with and marry indigenous women soon after they arrived in the Americas. In the early years, children of those unions were usually raised in one culture – either European or Aboriginal. But as time passed, the offspring of mixed marriages began to combine elements of both cultures, to produce something original – new Aboriginal peoples, the Métis.

Métis culture grew out of the circumstances of their lives. On the prairies, the language of the Métis – Michif (and its many dialects) – was a practical blend of French and several First Nations languages. Constant travel inspired portable art – exuberant song, dance and fiddle music and skilfully decorated clothing. Some Métis formed permanent settlements around trading centres. The buffalo hunt was an important organizing feature of other, more mobile Métis groups. For eastern Métis, a fishing economy shaped settlement patterns.

Using their family connections, their wilderness skills, and their knowledge of European and Aboriginal languages to extend European penetration into the North American interior, Métis people played a crucial role in building the country.

In Chapter 2, we defined the term nation and recommended a recognition policy for Aboriginal nations. The people of the western Métis Nation fit our criteria of nationhood. They have long been a culturally distinct people, they demonstrate social cohesiveness, and they have a record of political effectiveness. They might well be one of the first peoples to move toward nation status under the approach we propose. We expect that the Métis of Labrador and other Métis communities would follow suit, on a more extended timetable.

The government of Canada should deal with Métis people, like all other Aboriginal peoples, on a nation-to-nation basis. The *Constitution Act, 1982* already recognizes them as Aboriginal peoples, but the government has declined to extend most of its Aboriginal programs and services to them.

The government maintains that its responsibility for "Indians, and Lands reserved for the Indians", set out in section 91(24) of the *Constitution Act, 1867*, does not include the Métis. We disagree. More than 50 years ago, the

I'm Métis... It's a cultural, historical issue, and it's a way of life issue. It's not what you look like on the outside. It's how you carry yourself around on the inside that is important, in your mind and your soul and your heart.
Delbert Majer
Saskatchewan Metis
Addictions Council
Regina, Saskatchewan

Supreme Court ruled that federal jurisdiction under section 91(24) includes Inuit. The government now offers most of its programs and services to them. It is unjust and unreasonable to withhold from Métis people the services and opportunities available to other Aboriginal peoples.

The general goals of Métis people are not very different from those of other Aboriginal people:

reinforcing their culture, assuming political responsibility for themselves, obtaining a viable land base for economic and cultural development, and ensuring that their children are healthy, well educated and ready to lead the nation in their turn.

A land base is particularly important because, except in Alberta, Métis people have no territory of their own. Vast tracts of land in the prairies were to have been distributed to them under the *Manitoba Act, 1870* and the *Dominion Lands Act* of 1879, by means of a system known as 'scrip'. But those who tried to collect the land they were owed encountered delays, inefficiency, stonewalling and outright scams.

Often the allocated land was so far distant from a claimant's home base that his only real option was to sell it for whatever he could get. Local land speculators were ready and willing to buy – at bargain basement prices.

Moreover, the scrip system was not intended to result in a true Métis land base. Scrip was given to individuals, entitling them to settle with their families on discrete parcels of land. It was nothing like the reserve system, where First Nations shared an exclusive territory. The government of the day feared the growing numbers, economic strength and fire power of Métis people and aimed to break up their collectivities.

This history of sharp dealing has led the Métis of the prairies to argue that their land rights have never been extinguished. Métis in other parts of the country escaped the scrip debacle and now claim a land base in the general context of Aboriginal rights.

Aboriginal nationhood has always been closely connected to the land. To fulfil their legitimate social, cultural, political and economic aspirations, Métis people need their own land.

We urge federal, provincial and territorial governments to proceed rapidly with nation recognition so that Métis nation(s) can negotiate treaties or accords in the same manner as other Aboriginal peoples. These would specify the powers of their governments, the extent of their land base, the compensation owing to them for past injustices, their Aboriginal rights (such as the right to hunt, fish and trap on Crown land in all seasons), and the nature of their fiscal arrangements with other governments. These negotiations will be neither quick nor easy – all the more reason why they should begin now.

Métis people entered the twentieth century uprooted, fragmented and dispirited. They are determined that, as the next century unfolds, they will regain their rightful place as self-governing, self-sufficient, culturally vibrant Aboriginal people living in a more egalitarian Canadian society.

Voices from the North

Canada's North is home to Inuit, First Nations and Métis people and to non-Aboriginal people drawn there by the astonishing beauty of the North, its promise of economic opportunity, and the unique way of life it offers. It is a proving ground for political ideas and systems, a place where bold new initiatives can be tested. The North thus remains a place of exploration and discovery, of charting new paths and exploring new frontiers.

There has got to be a land and resource base for Métis. It's fundamental... There is a myth out there that when you talk land and resources that Métis may have less rights than some other Aboriginal people in this country... Our rights co-exist with the other Aboriginal peoples in this country.

Gary Bohnet
President, Metis Nation-
Northwest Territories

The Political Dimension

The Aboriginal peoples of the North live under a variety of political arrangements.

The 17 First Nation communities of the Yukon recently negotiated an Umbrella Final Agreement (UFA) that greatly increases their land and resource base and makes available a significant pool of capital for their use. The UFA also provides a framework for individual self-government agreements and, for the first time, does not require blanket extinguishment of Aboriginal title.

Dene signed two of the historical treaties, Treaty 8 and Treaty 11. As well, two contemporary land claims have been settled, one with the Gwich'in Dene and Métis, the other with the Sahtu Dene and Métis. The Dogrib are currently negotiating a third claim. Dene elsewhere in the North expect to achieve self-government through implementation of their treaties.

The Métis of northern Canada are not part of Treaties 8 and 11, but they are included in the two modern claims agreements that have been reached. They are seeking ways to restore and protect their rights in a combined process of constitutional development and land claims.

The 38,000 Inuit living in the North have exercised their right of self-determination through 'public government' (a form of governance discussed in Chapter 2). Eligibility to participate in governance is based on long-term residency, not Aboriginal nation or group membership. But because Inuit form a majority on their traditional territories, they can control government activity.

Most Inuit in the North share in one of three major land claims agreements: the James Bay and Northern Quebec Agreement, signed in 1975; the Inuvialuit Final Agreement (1984), covering the Inuvialuit in the western Arctic; and the *Nunavut Land Claims Agreement Act* and the *Nunavut Act* (1993), which will create a new territory in the eastern part of the Northwest Territories in 1999. Labrador is the only region settled mostly by Inuit that is without an agreement. The government has transferred adminis-

trative authority to Labrador Inuit in specific program areas, and they hope that a broader agreement can eventually be reached.

The pace of political change in the North over the last 20 years has been remarkable. People in all regions are settling in to build governing institutions that reflect the social and cultural variety of northern peoples.

Environmental Stewardship

Most Aboriginal northerners make their living in the 'mixed' economy. Households combine cash income from a variety of sources (employment, welfare, art and craft production) with hunting, fishing and other harvesting activities. As jobs come and go, as fish and fur prices rise and fall, as their circumstances change, people shift their mix of activities to match.

The health of the mixed economy depends on the health of the environment. Environmental stewardship is thus a matter of survival for northern Aboriginal peoples – survival of the mixed economy and their way of life.

Most northern Aboriginal people favour commercial development – but only if it happens

in ways that respect the land and all its life forms. However, the legacy of many resource extraction projects and of military installations that still dot the North has been extensive environmental damage.

Northerners speaking to the Commission expressed strong views about the need to clean up these sites and prevent future pollution; to improve the operations of regulatory bodies; and to use Aboriginal knowledge of natural phenomena to ensure sustainable resource use.

Initiatives such as wildlife co-management boards, which bring the combined expertise of Aboriginal hunters and non-Aboriginal scientists to bear on protection and harvesting issues, are an example of a northern approach to environmental stewardship that should be promoted and extended.

Supporting the Northern Economy

Even with a healthy environment, a question remains: how will all the people of the North make a living in the future? The adult population

The Aboriginal people are, by tradition, people of the land. Their very nature is tied strongly to the land and any answer to the economic problems must include their remaining on the land.
Rae Stephensen
Old Crow, Yukon

will grow significantly over the next decade, out-stripping the most optimistic forecast of new jobs. The cost of living is high, and public spending will not be able to meet all needs.

Aboriginal people can and should play a larger role in designing measures to increase self-reliance among those who, because of their circumstances, may always need income supplements of some kind. Programs that draw on Aboriginal values, self-awareness and creativity will have far more positive effects on those who need help than current programs have.

For example, funds from social assistance programs could be used to support traditional harvesting or paid labour of all kinds. In either case, the community would benefit from promoting self-reliance.

Our report also contains proposals for supporting the wage sector. Aboriginal people in the North have never shared fully in the economic benefits of resource extraction in their traditional territories. We describe ways for non-resident businesses and industries to give back something of what they are taking out of the North – by

recruiting more Aboriginal employees, helping to develop a more skilled labour force, supporting local businesses, and engaging in more joint ventures with Aboriginal people, communities and nations.

Taking Charge

Aboriginal people's way of life has been transformed in the past two decades. Where once they moved freely on the land, most now live in settled communities. Where once they had the independence – and the insecurity – of small hunter-gatherer societies, most now depend on wage employment or social assistance.

For some, the result has been a breakdown of traditional norms and values and in the responsible social behaviour that grew from them. Many northerners trace the abuse of alcohol and other social problems to the pace and scale of the changes they have experienced.

We support their intention to take charge of the institutions, processes and programs that will direct and control change in the North. This will allow them to work toward new codes of responsible social behaviour and new ways of sharing the frontier that is also their homeland.

VOICES OF URBAN ABORIGINAL PEOPLE

Almost half of all the Aboriginal people in Canada live in urban areas, and as many Aboriginal people live in Winnipeg as in the entire Northwest Territories. Many Canadians will find these facts surprising, and governments certainly appear to have given them little thought in policy and program decisions.

This information and policy vacuum can be traced, at least in part, to long-standing ideas about where Aboriginal people 'belong'. Canadians and their governments seem to believe that Aboriginal people were not meant for city life – or that, if they come to the city, they should live like 'ordinary Canadians'.

But culture is not something Aboriginal people discard at the city limits. The cultures in which people are raised and given their identity reside deep inside them and shape every aspect of being – wherever they happen to be living.

Who Are Urban Aboriginal People?

Some 320,000 self-identified Aboriginal people live in cities – that's 45 per cent of the total Aboriginal population, and the proportion is expected to grow.

Aboriginal people come to the city for many reasons. Often they seek new opportunity – education, a job, a chance to improve their lives. Some women leave home to escape abuse. Others are denied residence in their home communities (Bill C-31 notwithstanding). Whatever the reasons, Aboriginal women outnumber men in the urban population.

The city does not always keep its promise of a better life for Aboriginal people. They are markedly disadvantaged in comparison to their non-Aboriginal neighbours. In general they have less education, are less likely to have jobs, and are more likely to be poor.

The Question of Identity

Aboriginal people face an enormous struggle to maintain culture and identity in urban settings – let alone pass them on to their children. City life, with its myriad cultures and lifestyles, does not necessarily validate theirs. Episodes of racism lead many to question their identity and self-worth. Some told us they fear losing themselves, or they feel torn between worlds. Others repudiate their identity by denying their aboriginality or falling into self-destructive behaviour.

In our view, Aboriginal people should be able to feel at home and find affirmation of their identity wherever they choose to live. For Aboriginal culture to survive in cities, thriving communities are needed, with culture-based institutions to serve and support them.

In our public hearings, friendship centres were often described as places where any Aboriginal person can find support and acceptance in the city. The centres have long experience in delivering cultural education and rediscovery programs, and they should have secure funding from the federal government to carry on their work.

In some cities, Aboriginal people have opened their own schools, with cultural survival

Culture is not something Aboriginal people discard at the city limits.

The most effective way to catch these problems before they start is through strengthening an individual's identity and awareness of the community that exists in the city.

David Chartrand
President, National
Association of
Friendship Centres

as a main goal. In addition to subjects set by the provincial curriculum, they teach Aboriginal languages, history and traditions. Elders are normally involved, an important connection for youth in the absence of the extended family.

As discussed in Chapter 3, Aboriginal child and family service agencies are also becoming more common. With their policies of in-culture child placement where possible, they are also a bulwark against the gradual assimilation of urban Aboriginal people.

Unfortunately, governments offer an uneven checkerboard of programs and services for Aboriginal people in cities. They usually have only short-term or pilot project funding and are limited to a few aspects of life, such as housing and daycare.

We propose that all levels of government co-operate to increase support for cultural survival initiatives. The ideas are many, but funding has been all too meagre.

A Question of Responsibility

Many of the problems described by urban Aboriginal people stem from the lack of a co-ordinated approach to their concerns. They do not receive the same level of services and benefits from the federal government as First Nations people and Inuit living in their home communities (even if they have Indian status). Yet they face obstacles to using the provincial programs available to everyone.

The federal government usually takes the position that, once they have left their reserves or settlements, Aboriginal people are no longer a federal responsibility. Yet some provincial authorities argue that status Indians remain the responsibility of the federal government.

In our view, the federal government should be responsible for

- initiatives related to the emergence and operations of urban Aboriginal governments;
- services arising from treaty entitlements beyond those normally provided by provinces;

Self-determination for individuals and families is the foundation of Aboriginal people both on and off reserve.

Dan Smith
President, United
Native Nations
Vancouver,
British Columbia

■ any special services for urban Métis people, beyond those provided by the provinces, that may be agreed in future self-government negotiations.

Provincial and territorial governments are responsible for making the full array of general programs and services accessible to all Aboriginal people in urban areas, regardless of status. Where numbers warrant, provincial and territorial governments must ensure that their services are culturally appropriate.

We also see a need for enriched or remedial services, to help Aboriginal people achieve a quality of life similar to that of other urban Canadians. This cost should be shared by federal, provincial and territorial governments, according to a formula reflecting the fiscal capacity of each.

We would like to see urban services delivered on a 'status-blind' basis. That is, they should be available and accessible to all Aboriginal people, regardless of their nation of origin. In some provinces, however, urban services are being

delivered to First Nations and Métis people separately. Where this system is working well, we see no reason to disrupt it.

Self-Government in the City

One of the toughest issues in the urban context is self-government. It is fairly easy to imagine self-government in Aboriginal communities with a discrete land base. But what does it mean in cities? Will there be 'Aboriginal zones', with their own laws and governments?

We identified three possible approaches to self-government in urban areas:

■ The first involves the reform of local government services, to ensure Aboriginal influence. It would require guaranteed Aboriginal representation on boards and agencies whose activities directly affect Aboriginal people. Cities with a large Aboriginal population would establish Aboriginal affairs committees to give advice and guidance and co-management arrangements for the programs and services of greatest significance to Aboriginal residents.

■ Under the second approach, urban communities of interest would operate some govern-

Structures don't make change – people do.

ment services (schools, daycare centres, housing services) for themselves. A community of interest is an Aboriginal collectivity that has emerged over time in an urban setting, through voluntary association of people from different Aboriginal backgrounds. Its members could design and control their own city-wide institutions, with an umbrella political structure to oversee and co-ordinate activities.

■ The third approach is the nation-based approach. Many Aboriginal people have strong ties to their traditional lands and nations of origin and want a form of self-government with roots at home. For this approach to work, Aboriginal nations would have to take responsibility for their members who live in cities. Where Aboriginal nations accept this responsibility, they could establish urban branches of their home-based services and programs.

In addition, particularly in the west, there could be specific Métis services and agencies,

arranged in an interlocking network of decision-making bodies at the local, regional, provincial and national levels.

These and other approaches discussed in our report will take time to work out. The idea of urban self-government is only beginning to take shape, and most of the conceptual development should be done by Aboriginal people. We urge that governments, both non-Aboriginal and Aboriginal, co-operate to provide support in the planning stages and recognize viable urban governments as they emerge.

Because Aboriginal and non-Aboriginal people live as neighbours in urban areas, Canada's cities offer many chances for building bridges between cultures. We would like to see more Canadians initiate such activities.

Our relationships need to evolve [back] into a partnership...people-to-people, culture-to-culture, nation-to-nation. That is the direction we need to take.

Al Ducharme
Métis history teacher
La Ronge, Saskatchewan

RECOGNIZING DIVERSITY

As we talked to Aboriginal people all over Canada, we recognized – in some cases, for the first time – the enormous diversity among them. They do not make up a single-minded, monolithic entity, speaking with one voice. Canadians do not expect non-Aboriginal leaders to agree among themselves. They should not expect Aboriginal leaders to do so either.

Aboriginal people spring from many nation traditions. Their languages, belief systems and outlooks differ from one another in important respects – although they share much as well. They differ also in their experience of life in Canada – by age, by region and by location.

The diversity of Aboriginal perspectives and outlooks is a reality that other Canadians must accept, for the sake of greater understanding across the cultural divide. Aboriginal people themselves are struggling to come to terms with it, as they strive to build bridges across their dif-ferences so that they can use their combined voices to their collective benefit.

The importance of recognizing diversity for public policy is this: no one answer will do for all Aboriginal people. No one model – be it self-government, healing centre or housing design – will speak to all Aboriginal nations. Just as there are many voices, there must be many responses.

The ability to construct an identity for the self, either as an individual or as a collective, lies at the heart of modernity. I now see a group of [Aboriginal] people who are constructing a positive identity for themselves, who now see themselves as an integral part of, and contributors to, the society around them.

David Newhouse
Trent University

GRANNY TEACHES GRANDCHILDREN   COOP PROOF   E. KLENGENBERG 1992

Renewal: A Twenty-Year Commitment

5

Our report contains hundreds of recommendations. As our mandate directed, we looked at all the major problems facing Aboriginal people in their relationship with Canada. Each has proved difficult to resolve. Together they look even more unmanageable. Or so we thought when we began our work.

As we delved deeper, we came to appreciate the Commission's unique opportunity to approach the relationship between Canada and First Peoples in a new way – holistically. We realized that the usual strategy – tackling the problems one at a time, independently – is tantamount to putting a band-aid on a broken leg. Instead we propose a comprehensive agenda for change.

We talk at some length about new structures of governance, new strategies for economic devel-opment, new kinds of social programs. But at heart, what we want to do is something more radical. It is to bring about change in human lives. It is to ensure that Aboriginal children grow up knowing that they matter – that they are pre-cious human beings deserving love and respect, and that they hold the keys to a future bright with possibilities in a society of equals.

This is the goal of the Commission's agenda for change. The challenge remains: how to begin?

Foundations of a New Relationship

The starting point is recognition that Aboriginal people are not, as some Canadians seem to think, an inconsequential minority group with problems that need fixing and outmoded attitudes that need modernizing. They are unique political entities, whose place in Canada is unlike that of any other people.

Because of their original occupancy of the country, the treaties that recognized their rights, the constitution that affirms those rights, and their continued cohesion as peoples, they are nations within Canada – collectivities with their own character and traditions, a right to their own autonomous governments, and a special place in the flexible federalism that defines Canada.

Seeking a better balance of political and economic power between Aboriginal and other Canadian governments was the core and substance of our work. Progress on other fronts, unless accompanied by this transformation, will simply perpetuate a flawed status quo.

Throughout our report, we emphasize the importance of an understanding of history. We cannot expect to usher in a new beginning unless we reckon first with the past.

We do not propose dwelling on the past. Neither Aboriginal nor non-Aboriginal people want that. But there must be an acknowledgement that great wrongs have been done to Aboriginal people.

There is little evidence of such an acknowledgement today. Indeed, just as the restoration of Aboriginal nations and cultures appears to be offering real hope for renewed well-being, a backlash is developing – a reaction characterized by slogans like 'all Canadians are equal' and 'no special status' – but its premises are very wrong.

It is wrong to suggest that all people should be treated the same, regardless of inequalities in their situation.

It is wrong to turn a blind eye to the dispossession and racism that distort the circumstances of Aboriginal people and limit their life chances.

It is wrong to ignore the historical rights that Aboriginal people still enjoy as self-governing polit-

---

Remaining passive and silent is not neutrality – it is support for the status quo.

ical entities – rights that Canada undertook to safeguard as we were struggling toward nationhood.

Proponents of the so-called 'equality' approach claim that renewal and restoration in the ways we propose will bring 'apartheid' to Canada. In the name of equality, they would deny Aboriginal people the chance to protect their distinctive cultures and fashion their societies in ways that reflect their values.

This way of thinking is the modern equivalent of the mind-set that led to the *Indian Act*, the residential schools, the forced relocations – and the other nineteenth-century instruments of assimilation.

We ask those who think this way to reconsider their position. Its consequences are the very antithesis of equality, for it will freeze the existing imbalance of power and well-being between Aboriginal and non-Aboriginal people firmly in place.

We have survived Canada's assault on our identity and our rights... Our survival is a testament to our determination and will to survive as a people. We are prepared to participate in Canada's future – but only on the terms that we believe to be our rightful heritage.
Wallace Labillois
Council of Elders
Kingsclear, New Brunswick

Like our ancestors, we regard the right to be different not as an obstacle but as a foundation for our coexistence as distinct peoples.
Anthony Mercredi
Grand Chief, Treaty 8

A Word About the Constitution

Our agenda for change, though extensive and far-reaching, should not require constitutional amendment to become a reality. Aboriginal nations are free to act now on some of our proposals. In general, however, the best way to implement the new relationship is through government-to-government negotiations – within the existing constitutional framework.

But negotiations cannot be guaranteed to work. Nor has the Supreme Court provided guidance yet by ruling on the nature of Aboriginal self-government powers encompassed by the *Constitution Act, 1982*. Constitutional amendment, for the sake of clarity and certainty on key matters, is therefore appealing.

We also believe it is right and proper for the constitution to include a fully developed statement of the place of Aboriginal peoples in the federation.

There have been several attempts in the past two decades to rectify this omission – the amendments of 1982 and 1983, the constitutionally mandated first ministers conferences on Aboriginal matters (1983 to 1987), and the failed Charlottetown Accord. Regrettably, the omission remains.

When constitutional issues are again the subject of intergovernmental negotiation, the following Aboriginal issues must be included:

- explicit recognition that section 35 of the *Constitution Act, 1982* includes the inherent right of self-government as an Aboriginal right
- a process for honouring and implementing treaty obligations
- a veto for Aboriginal peoples on amendments to sections of the constitution that directly affect their rights – section 91(24) of the *Constitution Act, 1867* and sections 25, 35 and 35.1 of the *Constitution Act, 1982*
- recognition that section 91(24) includes Métis people along with First Nations and Inuit
- constitutional protection for the Alberta *Metis Settlements Act*
- changes to section 91(24) to reflect the broad self-governing jurisdiction Aboriginal nations can exercise as an inherent right and to limit federal powers accordingly

The statement of Canada's nationhood made by the constitution will never be complete until the relationship of respect and equality between Aboriginal and non-Aboriginal people that we envisage is represented there.

How to Begin

The first step is for the government of Canada to make a clear commitment to renewing the relationship between Aboriginal and non-Aboriginal people, guided by the principles of recognition, respect, sharing and responsibility.

Change of this magnitude cannot be achieved by piecemeal reform of existing programs and services – however helpful any one of these reforms might be. It will take an act of national intention – a major, symbolic statement of intent, accompanied by the laws necessary to turn intentions into action.

This can best be done by a new Royal Proclamation, issued by the Queen as Canada's head of state and the historical guardian of the rights of Aboriginal peoples, and presented to the people of Canada in a special assembly called for the purpose.

The proclamation would set out the principles of the new relationship and outline the laws and institutions necessary to turn those principles into reality. It would not supplant but support

and modernize the *Royal Proclamation of 1763*, which has been called Aboriginal peoples' *Magna Carta*.

The new proclamation would commit the government of Canada to making good on its proclaimed intentions by introducing new laws and institutions to implement them. The laws and institutions would come into being through companion legislation passed by Parliament:

■ An Aboriginal Nations Recognition and Government Act, to permit the government of Canada, following processes and criteria set out in the act, to recognize Aboriginal nations and make interim arrangements to finance their activities.

■ An Aboriginal Treaties Implementation Act, to establish processes and principles for recognized nations to renew their existing treaties or create new ones. This act would also establish several regional treaty commissions to facilitate and support treaty negotiations, which would be conducted by representatives of the governments concerned.

■ An Aboriginal Lands and Treaties Tribunal Act, which would establish an independent

On the blackboard: SOCIAL PROBLEMS: DRUG/ALCOHOL PROBLEMS — ABUSE

federal governing institutions and advise Parliament on matters affecting Aboriginal people. (A constitutional amendment, to come later, would create a House of First Peoples, to become part of Parliament along with the House of Commons and the Senate.)

■ An Aboriginal Relations Department Act and an Indian and Inuit Services Department Act, to set up two departments to replace the Department of Indian Affairs and Northern Development – one to implement the new relationship with Aboriginal nations, the second to administer continuing services for groups that have not yet opted for self-government.

The proclamation and companion legislation can be initiated by the federal government acting on its own. But it would be better for the future of the relationship and for the negotiations that lie ahead if the governments of Canada, the provinces, the territories and the Aboriginal nations were to work together from the very beginning.

We propose that close consultations with

body to decide on specific claims, ensure that treaty negotiations are conducted and financed fairly, and protect the interests of affected parties while treaties are being negotiated.

■ An Aboriginal Parliament Act, to establish a body to represent Aboriginal peoples within

Aboriginal peoples and provincial governments on the content of the proclamation and companion legislation begin within six months of the publication of this report.

Provincial and territorial governments have benefited greatly from Aboriginal peoples' loss of lands and resources. They have a moral and a legal responsibility to participate fully in measures to restore self-reliance and autonomy, including land redistribution, the redesign of government responsibilities, and arrangements for co-management of shared resources.

To this end, we call for a meeting of first ministers and Aboriginal leaders to be convened as soon as possible, but no later than six months after publication of our report. Its purpose will be to review our central recommendations, consult on the proposed Royal Proclamation, and set up a forum of ministers and representatives of key Aboriginal organizations to work out a Canada-wide framework agreement for negotiating key elements of the agenda for change, especially

- principles to guide redistribution of land and resources
- the general scope of Aboriginal governments' core jurisdiction
- principles of intergovernmental fiscal arrangements
- principles of co-management on public lands
- the character of interim relief agreements

This framework would significantly speed the process and lower the cost of the treaty negotiations to follow. The forum should have a target date of the year 2000 to complete its work.

GATHERING STRENGTH AND BUILDING CAPACITY

To this point we have discussed structural measures to rebalance power between Aboriginal peoples and Canadian governments. But structures don't make change; people do. Aboriginal people must regain hope that their rights will be recog-

If the wealth of our homelands is equitably shared with us, and if there is no forced interference in our way of life, we could fully regain and exercise our traditional capacity to govern...

Vice-Chief John McDonald
Prince Albert Tribal
Council
La Ronge, Saskatchewan

PEOPLE TO PEOPLE, NATION TO NATION

nized and their legacy of disadvantage over-
turned. When they do, their energies will be lib-
erated to fashion the thousands of individual
solutions that will make change a reality.

To equip Aboriginal people for the tasks of
nation building that lie ahead, structural change
– new laws, new bodies to implement them –
must be accompanied by measures to give people
hope, new capacities for self-management, and
the confidence to take charge in their communities and nations.

This requires early action in four areas: healing, economic development, human resources
development, and Aboriginal institution building.

■ Healing of individuals, families, communities and nations

Healing aims to restore physical, mental, emotional and spiritual health. It implies recovery for
individuals and communities from the wounds of
culture loss, paternalistic and sometimes racist
treatment, and official policies of domination
and assimilation.

Healing is already under way in many communities, but the momentum needs to grow. It

needs to be supported by schools, hospitals, family services. It needs to reach the young, the old,
and everyone in between.

Healing must build on Aboriginal traditions
of mutual aid and community responsibility. It
should include community and national leaders,
whose approaches to decision making are sometimes distorted by their experiences of government under the *Indian Act*. Restoring
communities and nations to unity and harmony
is an extension of healing at the personal level.
Such healing must accompany self-government.

■ Economic development

Aboriginal people must have the tools to escape
from the poverty that cripples them as individuals and as nations. Redistributing lands and
resources will greatly improve their chances for
jobs and a reasonable income. After that, the
tools most urgently needed are capital for investment in business and industry and enhanced
technical, management and professional skills to
realize new opportunities.

Hand in hand with improved economic conditions must come improved living conditions.
We propose a major initiative to bring housing,

We cannot become the independent
people we want to be and that we
have a right to be without access to
the resources of this very affluent
country.

Sophie Pierre
Ktunaxa/Kinbasket
Tribal Council
Cranbrook,
British Columbia

water supplies and sanitation facilities up to standards that will reduce threats to health and help restore self-respect and initiative.

■ Accelerating development of human resources

Activities of self-government, healing, community infrastructure development, and commercial enterprise will need many more trained people than are now available. Changes in the education system can generate better high school completion rates among Aboriginal students.

We also propose a 10-year initiative to overcome education and training deficits by involving private companies, training institutions and governments in programs to encourage Aboriginal people to develop skills in a full range of technical, commercial and professional fields.

■ Institution building

Most of the institutions governing Aboriginal life today originate outside Aboriginal communities. For the most part, they operate according to rules that fail to reflect Aboriginal values and preferences. In every sector of public life, there is a need to make way for Aboriginal institutions. Development of many of these institutions should proceed before self-governing nations emerge, but they should be designed to complement, not compete with, nation structures.

THE HIGH COST OF THE STATUS QUO

The case for a new deal for Aboriginal peoples rests on strong arguments for restorative justice and recognition of historical Aboriginal rights. It also rests on solid economic ground: Canada can no longer afford the status quo.

Eliminating the excess cost to Canadians of the policies of the past is a powerful argument for implementing the Commission's agenda for change.

■ The cost of Aboriginal peoples' inability to obtain good jobs and earn reasonable incomes is very high. It takes the form of earnings Aboriginal people never receive, goods and services they do not add to the economy, and taxes they cannot pay.

We have to be allowed to make our own mistakes. We have to be allowed to fall down from time to time and pick ourselves up. That's part of the process of being able to govern yourselves as a people and as a nation.

Gerald Morin
President, Métis
National Council

A smaller but still significant financial burden on taxpayers arises from the cost of remedial services to help Aboriginal people cope with the negative effects of their history of domination: higher than average use of welfare programs, housing subsidies, health and justice services.

Lost Earnings and Production

More than two-thirds of the cost of the status quo comes about because Aboriginal people are more likely than other Canadians to be unemployed and, when employed, they are likely to receive lower wages.

As a group, Aboriginal people are on the margins of the Canadian economy. They produce less, and thus contribute less than the average Canadian, to the wealth of the nation. Because they earn less, they have a substantially lower standard of living than other Canadians.

In 1990, only 43 per cent of Aboriginal people over age 15 had jobs, compared to 61 per cent of all Canadians.

In 1991, Aboriginal people who were employed earned $21,270 on average, or 76 per cent of the Canadian average of $27,880.

If these disparities did not exist, Aboriginal people would have added an additional $5.8 billion in goods and services to the Canadian economy in 1996. This is not a passing phenomenon. Substantial losses have been incurred for a long time. In the decade between 1981 and 1991, they actually increased.

The unemployment rate for Aboriginal people soared during that decade – far outpacing the increase for Canadians generally – and their average income declined. This happened despite a narrowing of the gap in educational attainment between Aboriginal and non-Aboriginal Canadians. This trend has likely continued through the '90s, as the influx of young people into the labour market and the lack of jobs have persisted.

This situation brings much suffering to Aboriginal people and communities and adds greatly to public indebtedness. More than 150,000 Aboriginal adults do not know the satisfaction of earning an adequate income and being economically independent.

Poverty, poor health, under-education and high mortality rates all indicate the long-term impacts of the colonization mind-set. It is the Aboriginal peoples' conception of their needs and interests which must be the starting point – the real [meaning] of the term 'self-determination'.
Marlene Buffalo
Hobbema, Alberta

Cost of Government Assistance

In 1992-93, the latest year for which information
on all governments is available, the federal government spent $6 billion dollars for Aboriginal
people, mostly on programs for registered Indians
and Inuit. Other governments (mainly the
provinces) spent $5.6 billion – for a total of
$11.6 billion.

Governments spend money on all citizens,
mostly on programs to provide health care and
education, stimulate the economy, facilitate
transportation and so on. But the amount spent
per person for Aboriginal people is 57 per cent
higher than for Canadians generally.

Why? Some of the federal government's
expenditures arise from special programs, such as
non-insured health benefits and post-secondary
education, that originate in treaty rights or
Indian Act obligations. Geography and demogra-
phy play a role as well:

■ The cost of delivering services to remote
regions, where many Aboriginal people live,
is high. For instance, the cost of delivering
services by the government of the Northwest
Territories is twice the national level.

■ Rapid growth in the Aboriginal population
makes some higher spending inescapable.
For example, the age structure of the
Aboriginal population makes expenditures
on education twice as high as for Canadians
generally.

Other factors relate to Aboriginal people's
social and economic conditions, which inflate the
need for some programs and services:

■ Aboriginal people are over-represented
among clients of remedial services such as
health care, social services and the justice system (policing, courts and jails).
■ High and rising rates of poverty and unemployment increase the need for welfare, housing subsidies and other payments to
individuals.

Costs incurred because of geography and
population growth are unavoidable. But a large
portion of the cost of individual assistance and
remedial health and social programs could be

eliminated – with the right policy alternatives.

The excess cost of assistance to Aboriginal people – that is, the amount over and above what is spent on an equivalent number of other Canadians – is estimated at $2.5 billion for 1996. (This figure consists of $0.8 billion for financial assistance and $1.7 billion for remedial programs.)

The tax dollars lost because of unemployment and low-wage employment is estimated at $2.1 billion for 1996. When this amount is added to the $2.5 billion, a figure of $4.6 billion emerges as the cost to Canadian governments of continuing policy failure with respect to Aboriginal people. This is about how much the government of New Brunswick spends to run the entire province for a year.

We can go further. Potential earnings lost to Aboriginal people because of their depressed employment status and wages are estimated at $2.9 billion for 1996. Adding this to the $4.6 billion already lost produces a figure of $7.5 billion – the total cost to Canada of leaving

TABLE I
COST OF THE STATUS QUO – TODAY AND TOMORROW

	1996	2016
	($ billions)	
Cost to Aboriginal People		
Forgone earned income	5.8	8.6
Income taxes forgone	-2.1	-3.1
Financial assistance from governments	-0.8	-1.2
Net income loss of Aboriginal people	2.9	4.3
Cost to Governments		
Expenditures on remedial programs	1.7	2.4
Financial assistance to Aboriginal people	0.8	1.2
Government revenue forgone	2.1	3.1
Total cost to governments	4.6	6.7
Total cost of the status quo	7.5	11.0

Notes:
1. The cost of the status quo is shown in *italics*. Other figures show how this cost is distributed.
2. Most of the cost of forgone earned income ($5.8 billion in 1996) is borne by Aboriginal people in the form of lost income. The rest is borne by governments in the form of taxes forgone and various forms of assistance paid out. These costs to governments are not included in the amount given for 'Cost to Aboriginal People'.

Aboriginal people's social and economic circumstances as they are.

Unless Canada makes fundamental changes, these figures will increase substantially. If current trends continue, the yearly economic loss to Canada will rise from $7.5 billion to $11 billion (in 1996 dollars) over the next 20 years, in response to population increase alone (see Table 1).

RENEWAL AS A GOOD INVESTMENT

The Commission's agenda for change can substantially reduce the costs of Aboriginal marginalization, ill health and social distress. But changes of such magnitude will not be easy. Profound problems require solutions that deal with the root causes. Solutions, once identified and implemented, take time to come to fruition.

Canada stands to gain by acting on our proposals. Aboriginal people will gain by achieving greater productivity and higher incomes. Other Canadians will gain through reduced government spending and increased government revenues. Political, economic and social renewal can help Canada balance its books.

Our proposals will cost money, but they will also save money. Eventually, savings and new tax revenues will equal and then exceed the cost of the

strategy. We estimate that it will take between 15 and 20 years of investment to reach that point.

Accordingly, we recommend strongly that governments increase their annual spending, so that five years after the start of the strategy, spending is between $1.5 and $2 billion higher than it is today, and that this level be sustained for some 15 years.

In considering the increased outlay we recommend, Canadians should keep four things in mind:

- The agenda for change will cost Canada significantly less than a continuation of the status quo, amended piecemeal here and there. The price tag on lost productivity and remedial measures to make up for poverty and other forms of disadvantage is four to five times higher than the cost of the measures we propose.
- Our recommendations constitute an interactive strategy. To work, they must reinforce each other. Implementing self-government and acquiring an increased land base will generate a powerful momentum for economic self-reliance. Economic well-being tends to improve health status. At the same time, progress in healing and education will produce stronger, more confident individuals with the skills and abilities to manage businesses and run governments.

By tackling the issue of dependency, by creating more independent people and communities, we will change the manner in which our communities function so that we will be contributing to the wealth not just of our communities, but of this country.
  Francis Frank
  Chief Councillor,
  Tla-O-Qui-Aht First
  Nation community
  Port Alberni,
  British Columbia

Changes will have to be negotiated with and implemented by Aboriginal people – in the way they choose. This means that the pace of change will be determined by the capacity of Aboriginal nations and communities to implement their chosen priorities – a capacity that is still developing.

Governments are reassessing their role in society and cutting back public spending. It would be a travesty of justice, however, if concerted and effective action to rectify the results of a history of dispossession were abandoned on grounds of fiscal restraint. A great debt is owing, and Canadians cannot, in good conscience, default on it.

We estimate that half the potential gain from better social and economic conditions could be realized within the 20-year investment period. Beyond that point, social and economic recovery will continue under their own momentum. Over

the 20-year period, the flow of financing should evolve in three stages:

- In the first five years, an immediate and major infusion of resources will be needed for all aspects of healing, economic stimulation, upgrading community infrastructure, and developing new institutions and human resources. By contrast, although structural reform will begin in these early years – nation building, recognition of self-government, and land and treaty processes – these activities will need only limited funding.
- At the end of the first five years, as more Aboriginal nations complete land and self-government negotiations, large outlays will be needed to settle land claims and implement self-government. Although we expect to see most claims settled within the next 20 years, the cost of land settlements will be spread out over a longer period.
- After about 10 years, Aboriginal people and nations will begin to close the gap in economic self-reliance and contribute more to the financing of governments. The need for remedial programs will fall. The point

where fiscal gains from our strategy begin to outstrip its costs will be reached within 20 years of the start of the strategy.

Table 2 presents a summary of the changing balance of costs and benefits to governments.

Federal, provincial, territorial and Aboriginal governments will need to assume a share of the additional cost of the agenda for change. But the costs we describe will be borne in part by Aboriginal governments and financed through their own taxation efforts.

Federal, provincial and territorial governments will benefit greatly in the long term from

- reduced expenditures once the agenda for change begins to alleviate debilitating and costly conditions of Aboriginal life
- increased tax revenues as more Aboriginal people living off Aboriginal nation territories have jobs and decent incomes and pay taxes

As Commissioners we urge our fellow Canadians to commit the required resources to the actions we describe, to close the economic gap

The costs [of settling Aboriginal grievances] seem to be considerable in light of today's restrictions on budgets. In terms of the costs that historical events have wrought upon the Shuswap people, the [price] we have paid has been far more significant than the [price] that the Canadian government and the Canadian public have paid for our lands and our resources.
Chief Nathan Matthew
Secwepemc Nation
Kamloops, British
Columbia

between Aboriginal and non-Aboriginal people by 50 per cent and improve social conditions in the next 20 years.

Perhaps it will take longer. But within the 20-year timeframe, enormous momentum for change can be generated. By 2016, Aboriginal people can be very much better off than they are today and moving steadily forward.

The result will be a large gain in human and financial terms for Aboriginal people – and, in the long term, much greater savings for all Canadians.

TABLE 2

CHANGES IN GOVERNMENT FINANCES AS A RESULT OF THE STRATEGY

Additional allocation in the year	2001	2016
Structural measures	($ millions)	
1. Tribunal and treaty commissions	50	50
2. Nation rebuilding	50	0
3. Nation governments	50	425
4. Land claims settlements	0	1000
Total for structural measures	150	1475
Social and economic measures		
Healing		
5. Education, youth and culture	300	150
6. Health care	100	(450)
7. Social services	100	(425)
8. Justice	25	(325)
Economic opportunity and living conditions		
9. Economic development	350	225
10. Income transfers	0	(250)
11. Housing and infrastructure	400	350
12. Human resource development	150	425
Total for social and economic measures	1,425	(300)
Government revenue gains	—	(1,550)
Overall total	1,575	(375)

Notes:

1. Positive entries (figures without parentheses) show the increase in spending by all governments needed to implement the strategy.

2. Reductions are shown by numbers in parentheses in the second column. These relate to amounts saved as a result of the strategy (that is, amounts that would be spent if the status quo continues) and to additional revenues collected by governments. See Volume 5, Chapter 3, of the Commission's report for a complete explanation of these figures.

3. Figures are rounded to the nearest $25 million.

AWARENESS AND UNDERSTANDING

The tasks we have laid out for renewing the relationship between Aboriginal and non-Aboriginal people are huge – but they pale in comparison to the task of changing Canadian hearts and minds so that the majority understand the aspirations of Aboriginal people and accept their historical rights.

Social and structural change will not take place unless Canadians want it to. Leadership from governments is necessary but not enough. People need to see the reasons for – and the justice in – the Commission's agenda for change. They must urge governments forward when they waver, and they must be ready to accommodate the set-backs and surprises that inevitably come with major change.

We were told many times during our mandate that most Canadians know little of Aboriginal life and less of Aboriginal history. Information in school curriculums is limited. Media coverage is often unsatisfactory. Few governments, agencies and organizations promote awareness of Aboriginal issues among members, employees and colleagues.

Yet without mutual understanding, a renewed relationship is impossible.

Part of the answer is information. We recommend a number of steps to increase and improve the quality of information about Aboriginal people and their concerns. But information alone will not break down walls of indifference and occasional hostility. Aboriginal and non-Aboriginal people need many more chances to meet each other face to face and learn about one another.

We urge Canadians to become involved in a broad and creative campaign of public education. Our report can be a starting point – a basis for study groups, lectures, meetings and exchanges, organized by churches and unions, schools and hospitals, local businesses and national corporations, about what they can do to understand and accommodate Aboriginal people and their concerns.

Remaining passive and silent is not neutrality – it is support for the status quo.

If...awareness is not increased dramatically, then the probability of [Métis] people assuming their rightful place in society in the future is very low.

Gerald Thom
Metis Nation of Alberta

CHARTING PROGRESS

Aboriginal people came before the Commission with a question: Can you promise us that your recommendations won't just gather dust on a shelf? Fine words are all too familiar to Aboriginal people. This time, they want them to be made real.

The Commission's agenda for change is, clearly, a long-term undertaking. It makes sense to monitor progress until those changes are accomplished.

We propose that the federal government set up an Aboriginal Peoples Review Commission to assess the actions of governments in accomplishing the tasks on the agenda for change.

The importance of an Aboriginal Peoples Review Commission will lie in its independence and its ability to focus the attention of legislators and governments on the continuing process of renewal. It should be independent of governments and report direct to Parliament.

I like to camp in the bush. I like the quietness and I like to go to the lodge. I like the school.

LAST WORDS

The relationship between Aboriginal and non-Aboriginal people in Canada has long been troubled and recently has shown signs of slipping into more serious trouble. The relationship can most certainly be mended – indeed, turned from a problem into an asset and one of the country's greatest strengths.

The direction change must take is toward freeing Aboriginal people from domination by and dependence on the institutions and resources of governments. The end of dependence is something Aboriginal and non-Aboriginal people alike profoundly desire. It would be quite unacceptable for First Nations, Inuit and Métis peoples to continue to find their autonomy restricted and constrained in the twenty-first century.

Yet renewal of the relationship must be done with justice and generosity. History and human decency demand restoration of fair measures of land, resources and power to Aboriginal peoples. On those foundations, self-respect and self-reliance will grow steadily firmer in Aboriginal communities. In their absence, anger and despair will grow steadily deeper – with conflict the likely result.

Aboriginal people must be enabled to function once again as nations. This is a new way of thinking about old and persistent problems. For many years, the watch-word for the progress of

What we propose
is fundamental,
sweeping and perhaps
disturbing – but also
exciting, liberating,
ripe with possibilities.

Aboriginal people was 'self-government'. But this is only one piece of a larger undertaking – the restoration of nations, not as they were, but as they can be today. Land and economic vitality are essential for successful, hard-working governments. Whole, healthy, hopeful people are more vital still.

The Commission proposes a 20-year agenda for change, encompassing these things and more. In just 20 years, the revitalization of many self-reliant Aboriginal nations can be accomplished, and the staggering human and financial cost of supporting communities unable to manage for themselves will end. From that time forward, the return to the country will continue to grow.

That so much is possible in so short a time is good news for Canadians.

The changes we propose are not modest. We do not suggest tinkering with the *Indian Act* or launching shiny new programs. What we propose is fundamental, sweeping and perhaps disturbing – but also exciting, liberating, ripe with possibilities.

Nor do we propose a set of lock-step directives. We offer a vision of what is possible and

lots of ideas about how to get started. The agenda for change can begin today, and there are many starting places for it. Indeed, it is already getting started, as good ideas take shape and gather momentum in Aboriginal communities from coast to coast to coast.

Yet change must take place at a pace that allows Aboriginal people and nations to work through the pains of rebirth and in a way that encourages non-Aboriginal people to participate in it. Transition is something we must do together.

All of us have a part in securing the new relationship – people and governments, Aboriginal and non-Aboriginal, organizations big and small. We have 20 years of building and experimentation to look forward to – using, for the first time in many decades, all the energies of Aboriginal people as they create and live the dream of a Canada that they can share with others and yet be fully at home.

During that time – and beyond it – we can look forward to a Canada that celebrates Aboriginal heritage and draws strength from Aboriginal peoples as full partners in a renewed federation.

To purchase the Commission's five-volume report, contact your local bookseller or

Canada Communication Group – Publishing
Ottawa, Ontario
K1A 0S9

A CD-ROM, containing the report, transcripts of the Commission's public hearings, reports and commentaries published during the Commission's mandate, and research studies, will also be available through the Canada Communication Group – Publishing at this address.

Credits:

Inside covers: Mireille Siouï, "Dans la maison d'Handiaouich, la petite tortue", intaglio, watercolour on paper, 50 X 32.5 centimetres.

Page xii: Joane Cardinal-Schubert, RCA, "Moonstruck I", acrylic on paper, 64.5 X 54 centimetres, framed.

Page 22: Roger Simon, "Raven Woman", oil on diamat paper, 66.5 X 56.5 centimetres, framed.

Page 58: Jim Logan, "The Visit", 1987, acrylic on canvas, 72 X 48 centimetres.

Page 98: Jane Ash-Poitras, "Buffalo Hierophany", 1992, mixed media, 105.5 cm X 75.5 cm, framed.

Page 124: Elsie (Klengenberg) Anaginak, "Granny Teaches Grandchildren", 1992, stencil print on Arches paper, 56 X 43 centimetres.

Page 146: Bob Boyer, "Mother Earth's June Berry Soup", oil and acrylic on flannel, 240.5 X 97.5 X 9 centimetres.

All, collection of the Indian Art Centre, Department of Indian Affairs and Northern Development. Photographer, Lawrence Cook.

Photography: Fred Cattroll, except for Makivik Corporation, front cover, 3rd from left, and pages 15, 35, 56, 73, 113, 115, 132, 149

Illustrations: Children of Fort Chipewyan, Alberta

Design: Miriam Bloom

Production: Donna Bates